Elements in the Philosophy of Biology
edited by
Grant Ramsey
KU Leuven

THE SCOPE OF EVOLUTIONARY THINKING

Thomas A. C. Reydon
Leibniz University Hannover

Shaftesbury Road, Cambridge CB2 8EA, United Kingdom

One Liberty Plaza, 20th Floor, New York, NY 10006, USA

477 Williamstown Road, Port Melbourne, VIC 3207, Australia

314–321, 3rd Floor, Plot 3, Splendor Forum, Jasola District Centre,
New Delhi – 110025, India

103 Penang Road, #05-06/07, Visioncrest Commercial, Singapore 238467

Cambridge University Press is part of Cambridge University Press & Assessment,
a department of the University of Cambridge.

We share the University's mission to contribute to society through the pursuit of
education, learning and research at the highest international levels of excellence.

www.cambridge.org
Information on this title: www.cambridge.org/9781009181846

DOI: 10.1017/9781009181839

© Thomas A. C. Reydon 2025

This publication is in copyright. Subject to statutory exception and to
the provisions of relevant collective licensing agreements, with the exception
of the Creative Commons version the link for which is provided below, no
reproduction of any part may take place without the written permission of
Cambridge University Press & Assessment.

An online version of this work is published at doi.org/10.1017/9781009181839
under a Creative Commons Open Access license CC-BY 4.0

When citing this work, please include a reference to the DOI 10.1017/9781009181839

First published 2025

A catalogue record for this publication is available from the British Library

ISBN 978-1-009-61919-6 Hardback
ISBN 978-1-009-18184-6 Paperback
ISSN 2515-1126 (online)
ISSN 2515-1118 (print)

Cambridge University Press & Assessment has no responsibility for the persistence
or accuracy of URLs for external or third-party internet websites referred to in this
publication and does not guarantee that any content on such websites is, or will
remain, accurate or appropriate.

For EU product safety concerns, contact us at Calle de José Abascal, 56, 1°, 28003
Madrid, Spain, or email eugpsr@cambridge.org

The Scope of Evolutionary Thinking

Elements in the Philosophy of Biology

DOI: 10.1017/9781009181839
First published online: September 2025

Thomas A. C. Reydon
Leibniz University Hannover

Author for correspondence: Thomas A. C. Reydon, reydon@ww.uni-hannover.de

Abstract: Evolutionary theory has found its way into a staggeringly large diversity of fields outside the biological sciences. This Element examines how crossovers of evolutionary theory from biology into other fields occur, and in what ways such fields can be meaningfully considered *evolutionary* fields of research. Cases of crossover of evolutionary theory have so far not been examined systematically by philosophers of science, and this Element aims to make a start with developing a philosophical account of this practice as a general strategy in science. It shows that theory crossovers do not consist in straightforward applications of a generally accepted version of evolutionary theory to non-biological phenomena, but must be understood differently. As an alternative account, it is suggested that crossovers of evolutionary theory involve a general style of thinking – evolutionary thinking – and it is shown how this provides a unifying perspective on crossovers of evolutionary theory between fields. This title is also available as Open Access on Cambridge Core.

Keywords: evolutionary thinking, evolutionary theory, evolutionary social science, evolutionary algorithms, generalized evolution

© Thomas A. C. Reydon 2025

ISBNs: 9781009619196 (HB), 9781009181846 (PB), 9781009181839 (OC)
ISSNs: 2515-1126 (online), 2515-1118 (print)

Contents

1 A Theory Travels   1

2 Crossover without Models   9

3 The Source Field: Evolutionary Theorizing in Biology   18

4 Three Modes of Crossover   35

5 The Evolutionary Style of Thinking   59

   References   69

1 A Theory Travels

1.1 Evolutionary Everything

Scientific theories sometimes travel far beyond the borders of the field in which they originated, not only finding their way into public discourse and sociopolitical views, but also into other academic fields of research. Evolutionary theory is a particularly striking case. More than any other scientific theory, Darwin's theory and its successors gave rise to ongoing debates on its potential implications for traditional worldviews, religious beliefs, personal morality, political and social ideologies, and so on.[1] And evolutionary theory is exceptional too in how widely and systematically it impacts areas of research and scholarship outside its home turf.

Since the late nineteenth century, numerous approaches and even entire fields of research have emerged that self-identify as "evolutionary" in titles of papers and books, and the names of journals, conferences, and societies. A prominent early proponent of an evolutionary approach outside biology was the English polymath Herbert Spencer, who coined the phrase "survival of the fittest" and envisioned an evolutionary social science based on a general theory of progressive evolution (Spencer, 1890; 1891: 8–62). Toward the end of the nineteenth century, the American economist and sociologist Thorstein Veblen coined the term "evolutionary economics" (Veblen, 1898) and, influenced by Spencer's work, argued that economics should incorporate elements of Darwin's thought. Around the same time, the American philosopher and psychologist William James coined the term "evolutionary psychology." James argued that psychological research should go beyond the observable manifestations of the mind and dig deeper into the biological roots of the mental: James argued that acknowledging the fact that mental phenomena depend on evolved physiological structures (the organism's nervous system) implies that "the psychologist is forced to be something of a nerve-physiologist" (1890: 5) who must consider the evolutionary history of the nervous system when studying the mind.

During the twentieth century, the number of approaches and fields that self-identify as "evolutionary" rapidly multiplied, causing philosopher of biology David Hull to comment somewhat scathingly that "[e]volutionary everything is hot right now" (Hull, 1998: 513) – a sentiment that was

---

[1] I will not consider these issues here, but see Midgley (2002), Dupré (2003), Ruse (2005; 2017), Buskes (2006), de Smedt & de Cruz (2020), and Desmond et al. (2024) for discussions of the relation between evolution, religion, and worldviews more broadly. See O'Connell & Ruse (2021) for a concise discussion of social Darwinism.

echoed later by philosopher of biology Werner Callebaut (2011: 103). Indeed, evolutionary approaches have found their way into a strikingly large array of academic fields. In the context of origins of life research, geochemists have since the 1950s been interested in the chemical evolution of self-replicating molecular systems (Calvin, 1965; Lemmon, 1970; Schoenmakers et al., 2024). Evolutionary epistemology arose in the 1960s–1970s as an attempt to understand human knowledge as a product of selective forces acting on competing units of knowledge (Gontier & Bradie, 2021; Bradie & Harms, 2023). A related line of research, which currently enjoys renewed attention from philosophers of science and technology, involves attempts to understand scientific and technological change as evolutionary processes (Basalla, 1988; Hull, 1988; Ziman, 2000; Brey, 2008; Smaldino & McElreath, 2016; Haufe, 2022; Smaldino, 2022; Charbonneau, 2024). A century after James' work, evolutionary psychology was joined by a clinical companion in the form of "Darwinian psychiatry" (McGuire & Troisi, 1998). Cosmology has a small research program that explores the hypothesis of cosmological natural selection (Smolin, 1992; Gardner & Conlon, 2013), and in quantum physics we find researchers pursuing "quantum Darwinism" (Zurek, 2009).

Any quick online search yields numerous hits on yet more evolutionary fields and approaches. These include evolutionary aesthetics, evolutionary anthropology, evolutionary archaeology, evolutionary computing, evolutionary criminology, evolutionary demography, evolutionary electronics, evolutionary ethics, evolutionary history, evolutionary jurisprudence, evolutionary linguistics, evolutionary literary studies (or "literary Darwinism"), evolutionary medicine, evolutionary nutrition science, evolutionary organization science, evolutionary physiology, evolutionary political science, evolutionary robotics, evolutionary sociology and more.[2] Some of these, such as evolutionary economics, evolutionary psychology, and evolutionary computing, have established themselves as thriving academic communities. Others, such as cosmological natural selection or literary Darwinism, remain somewhat esoteric outliers within their respective fields that may or may not gain traction.

Notwithstanding their self-identification as "evolutionary" or "Darwinian," these fields and approaches constitute a highly diverse group of research areas. Most importantly, they differ among each other in the ways in which they connect to evolutionary theory. Furthermore, some

---

[2] See Barkow (2006) and Desmond et al. (2024) for literature references for some of these fields.

highly visible fields, such as evolutionary economics and evolutionary psychology, are internally diverse and encompass multiple competing types of evolutionary approaches. Evolutionary economics, for example, encompasses a remarkable variety of approaches that differ with respect to how much they take from evolutionary theory and which elements they use (Nelson & Winter, 1982; Hodgson, 2009; 2019; Nelson, 2018; Schulz, 2020). According to Hodgson, for example, "[a]t best, 'evolutionary economics' is an umbrella term to describe a loose collection of theoretical approaches and empirical studies" (2009: xiii). Something similar has been said about evolutionary, or "Darwinian," archaeology (Maschner & Mithen, 1996: 11; Prentiss, 2021).

This situation raises important questions. What – if anything – do these fields and approaches have in common that would make them *evolutionary* in any meaningful sense of the term? Can a common explanatory strategy be found that would allow us to understand them as all producing evolutionary explanations of the phenomena they study? How do crossovers of evolutionary theory from biology into other fields occur? What types of crossover can be identified and how can they be justified? What exactly is it that crosses between fields? What kinds of epistemic work can evolutionary approaches perform in areas outside the biological sciences and where do they run into difficulties? And why are evolutionary approaches so appealing to non-biologists in the first place?

These questions have so far hardly been investigated systematically by philosophers of science. A few specific fields have been subject to extensive scrutiny: evolutionary psychology, for instance, has drawn considerable criticism from philosophers of science (e.g., Dupré, 2000; 2001; Buller, 2005; Lewens, 2015: 147ff.; Smith, 2020), and evolutionary economics is increasingly being examined (Schulz, 2020; André et al., 2022). But the general practice of transferring elements from evolutionary theory into non-biological fields has only recently begun to draw attention from philosophers of science (recent work includes Reydon & Scholz, 2009; 2014; 2015; Schurz, 2011; Brinkworth & Weinert, 2012; Scholz & Reydon, 2013; Heams et al., 2015; Koliofotis, 2021; Reydon, 2021; 2023; Baraghith & Feldbacher-Escamilla, 2021; Baraghith, 2022; Du Crest et al., 2023). Biologists also consider the topic, but only rarely (Bull & Wichman, 2001; Derry, 2009).

In this Element, I aim to clarify what potential answers could be to these questions. Providing answers to all these questions would be much too large a project for an Element, as would be an in-depth examination of all extant evolutionary fields and approaches. Instead, I will use specific cases to sketch the outlines of a general account of the crossover of evolutionary theory from biology into other fields that shows how crossovers occur, what exactly travels between fields in such cases, and in what ways the various approaches and fields mentioned earlier can be considered evolutionary. I will argue that what makes them evolutionary is *not* that they straightforwardly apply the same scientific theory to a broad range of problems in various fields. Rather, researchers usually employ heavily "flattened" accounts of the evolutionary process without much consideration for the actual richness and pluralism of biological evolutionary theorizing, and there is little shared theoretical content between the various fields.[3]

What makes such approaches evolutionary notwithstanding such flattening of theoretical content, I will suggest, is that they embody the same general *style of thinking* that orients itself on a particular kind of ideal scientific explanation. That ideal, in turn, is aimed at a particular kind of explanandum, namely those aspects of the forms of the various kinds of entities found in the world that cannot be explained completely as products of human design. This perspective, I believe, helps to clarify how evolutionary approaches can be used to explain a broad spectrum of phenomena outside biology, but also to highlight the difficulties that such approaches often face. Accordingly, this Element is intended as a critical survey of how evolutionary theory crosses between fields. It is aimed at a broad audience of philosophers of science, life scientists, and scholars and scientists in other areas who are interested in applying evolutionary approaches in their own field.

1.2 Situating the Project

The philosophical literature on evolutionary theory, the broad topic of "evolutionary everything," and on the crossover of theories between fields, is extensive. To situate the project that I pursue here within the relevant debates, let me clarify how my topic connects to other relevant topics that will largely remain in the background. This Element examines a special case of the practice of using parts of the theoretical structure of one field to explain and predict phenomena studied in another field of research – a widespread practice in science. Economists and social scientists, for example, have a long tradition of borrowing concepts and mathematical

---

[3] I use "flattened" to indicate that the picture of the evolutionary process used in instances of theory crossover typically lacks the richness and depth of the picture that evolutionary biology provides us with. For a similar criticism, see Callebaut (2011: 103).

formalisms from physics to describe and explain economic and social phenomena (Mayntz, 1992; Boumans, 1993; Yee, 2021). Similarly, elements taken from statistical physics have been used in the development of approaches in population genetics and evolutionary biology (Sella & Hirsh, 2005; Pence, 2021: 55–57).

Connections between the content of fields can be made in numerous ways, ranging from the metaphorical use of another field's terminology and the drawing of analogies between phenomena from different fields, via the transfer of models between fields, to attempts to reduce the explanatory theory of one field to a special case of the explanatory theory of another field. While all these ways of connecting fields occur with respect to evolutionary theory, for reasons of space I will only focus on a specific category of cases in which epistemic content – such as a scientific theory, a conceptual framework or a few concepts, a model, or an equation or set of equations – is taken from one field (the source field) and applied in another, often unrelated, field (the target field) to explain phenomena that are being investigated there.

Sociologist Renate Mayntz (1992; 1997a: 312–327; 1997b: 307–308; cf. Reydon, 2021) was one of the first authors to highlight this practice in relation to the application of theories from the natural sciences in the social sciences. Mayntz calls this practice "borrowing" or "theory transfer" and describes it as involving the transfer of theoretical components "ranging from single concepts to complete theoretical models" (Mayntz, 1992: 29) from a source domain into a target domain.

According to Mayntz, transferring a single concept from one field into another only yields "a mere semantic innovation that adds nothing to our substantive knowledge" (Mayntz, 1992: 65–66). The reason is easy to see: taking a central concept such as "natural selection" from an established theory and using it elsewhere amounts to taking the concept out of the theoretical context from which it derives its meaning and placing it within a new context in which it may well fail to do the explanatory or predictive work it is expected to perform. This is often the case when crossovers principally rely on analogical reasoning or on using concepts in a metaphorical manner. While analogies and metaphors perform important heuristic and communicative roles in science, they do not involve the actual transfer of epistemic content between fields.

For example, analogies often lie at the basis of modeling efforts (Frigg, 2023: 289ff.; Herfeld, 2025), but the *justification* of transferring a model between fields must go beyond the analogy. Specifying relevant similarities between distinct phenomena is merely the first step: for crossovers to have genuine explanatory and predictive force, they must involve close examination of the ontologies of the source and target fields to show that the similarity is sufficient to support the same kind of explanation in both domains (see Section 2). For this reason, I will not explicitly address the use of analogies and metaphors in crossovers of evolutionary theory. There is a considerable volume of literature on the role of analogies and metaphors in the development of biological evolutionary theory as well as on the use of evolutionary analogies and metaphors in areas outside the life sciences, to which I refer readers (e.g., Maasen et al., 1995; Beer, 2009; Schulz, 2020; Baraghith & Feldbacher-Escamilla, 2021; André et al., 2022).

Similar reasons apply to attempts to *reduce* biological evolution to more fundamental chemical or physical processes, and to the broad topic of cultural evolution. Attempts at reducing the process of biological evolution to more fundamental physical or chemical processes are comparatively rare. They are primarily found in origins of life research (see Charlat et al., 2023; Schoenmakers et al., 2024), but do not encompass transfers of epistemic content from biology into other fields and thus fall outside the topic of this Element.

Cultural evolution, too, does not always involve cases of genuine crossover of evolutionary theory into other fields. "Cultural evolution" does not denote a clearly delimited, unified field of research, but rather is an umbrella name for a variety of approaches to the study of human cultures, societies, language, behavior, and so on, not all of which are evolutionary in any strong sense (for discussions, see Mesoudi, 2011: 25ff.; Lewens, 2015; Prentiss, 2021). I take this as a reason to not discuss cultural evolution *as such*, that is, as if it were a homogeneous evolutionary field of research, a research program, or a single approach. As a topical domain, cultural evolution overlaps partially with many of the fields mentioned earlier, including evolutionary aesthetics, evolutionary archaeology, evolutionary linguistics, evolutionary psychology, evolutionary sociology, and the evolution of science and technology. But such overlaps remain partial and each field encompasses large areas of work that do not connect to approaches that count as falling within the domain of cultural evolution. Accordingly, cultural evolution will feature here only implicitly when in Section 4 I examine some of the evolutionary fields with which it partly overlaps. For concise philosophical analyses of cultural evolution, I refer readers to the literature that is already available (e.g., Lewens, 2015; 2024; Nichols et al., 2024).

Moreover, I am reluctant to interpret some of the most prominent evolutionary approaches in cultural evolution as crossovers of epistemic content in the sense examined in this Element. To see this, a distinction must be made between approaches that take facts about human evolutionary history to inform the study of human behavior and culture (which are discussed in Section 4.1) and approaches that study the *dynamics* of cultural evolution. The latter, I suggest, do not instantiate crossover. For example, Dual-Inheritance Theory or "gene-culture coevolution" (Cavalli-Sforza & Feldman, 1981; Boyd & Richerson, 1985; 2005; Mesoudi, 2011: 55–83), rests on the observation that in addition to genetic inheritance humans developed a second inheritance mechanism that transmits units of cultural information. This gives rise to a view of the human species as having two categories of traits, biological and cultural traits, that are transmitted by two inheritance systems that operate independently but mutually affect each other. The bearers of these traits still are individual humans or groups of humans, though, such that modern human evolution is understood here as biological evolution in a modified form. This approach thus is not so much a case of actual crossover of evolutionary theory into a non-biological field, but I believe is better characterized as the study of the dynamics of biological evolution as it manifests itself in one particular species (and probably in several closely related species too). I contend (but am unable to develop the argument here) that on the most recent developments in biological evolutionary theorizing (namely the "Extended Synthesis" discussed in Section 3.5; see, in particular, Jablonka & Lamb, 2005; 2020) Dual-Inheritance Theory could be subsumed under biological evolutionary theory that encompasses cultural inheritance as one of the mechanisms that occurs in the evolution of some species of organisms.

Finally, crossovers of evolutionary thinking are sometimes discussed under the header of (Universal) Darwinism (e.g., Nelson, 2007; Lewens, 2024) and many evolutionary fields self-identify as taking a (Neo-)Darwinian approach. But "Darwinism," "Darwinian," and cognate terms do not denote a clearly defined approach to evolutionary phenomena (Desmond et al., 2024) and using these terms to characterize approaches can obscure important differences between them.

Theory development after Darwin resulted in a diversity of accounts of evolution that to some extent can claim to be Darwinian (see Section 3). "Neo-Darwinism," for instance, was coined by Romanes (1895) to denote an ultra-selectionist version of Darwin's theory, which was promoted by Alfred Russel Wallace and differed in important respects from Darwin's own view (Romanes also called it "Ultra-Darwinism"). Today, however, "Neo-Darwinism" is often used to denote two later formulations of evolutionary theory, the Modern Synthesis and the Gene's-Eye

View, both much less selection-focused than Wallace's theory. To add to the confusion, Samuel Butler used "Neo-Darwinism" before Romanes to denote Charles Darwin's theory and to distinguish it from the views of Charles's grandfather, Erasmus Darwin, whose evolutionary theory Butler considered "the original Darwinism" (1880: 280).

"Universal Darwinism" was introduced by Richard Dawkins (1983) to denote the claim that biological evolution through natural selection is not confined to planet Earth but will occur in living systems anywhere in the universe – if extraterrestrial life exists. Dawkins' Universal Darwinism thus does not involve theory crossover as discussed here, and in fact Dawkins (2008) expressed caution against exporting evolutionary approaches outside biology overly enthusiastically. Analyzing crossovers as instances of (Universal) Darwinism crossing into new fields thus adds more confusion than clarity.

To show in what way crossovers of evolutionary theory constitute a special case of the practice of using parts of the theoretical structure of one field in another field, that differs in important ways from other cases, I first discuss how philosophers commonly understand theory crossover, namely in terms of formal models that are taken from one field and applied in another (Section 2.1). Section 2.2 then presents the argument in abbreviated form for my claim that the case of evolutionary theory is fundamentally different, and Section 3 deepens the argument. The argument is that in the case of evolutionary theory there are no models of evolution that could be transferred and make a target field into an evolutionary field of research. This raises the question what, then, it is exactly that is crossing between fields in the case of evolutionary theory of not general models of evolution.

I address this question by first examining the source of crossover, biological evolutionary theory (Section 3).[4] This will show that what is available for transfer into other fields is not a unified theory, but rather a deeply pluralistic way of understanding central aspects of the living world. I then survey the three main modes of crossover of evolutionary theory into fields outside biology (Section 4): using *evolutionary history* to bridge evolution with otherwise non-evolutionary research, using *evolutionary algorithms* to explore large design spaces, and using an *evolutionary explanatory framework* as a basis to develop an overarching explanatory

---

[4] Because this Element aims at a broad audience, I survey evolutionary theorizing in some – perhaps too much – detail. Yet, Section 3 cannot claim to be a complete overview, as I highlight points that are particularly relevant for the topic of this Element. Readers well versed in evolutionary theory may consider skimming this section.

theory covering phenomena in diverse fields.[5] Against this background I develop my account of evolutionary thinking as a style of thinking that underpins these modes of crossover (Section 5).

2 Crossover without Models

2.1 Model Transfer

While it is tempting to think of the "evolutionary" fields mentioned in Section 1 as involving the straightforward application of one of our best scientific theories – Darwinian evolutionary theory – to a wide range of non-biological phenomena in the same way as biologists apply the theory in its home domain, this is not what actually happens. Crossovers between fields do not involve entire theories but other epistemic entities – usually *models* – as the entities that travel between fields.[6] Most work in the philosophy of science on theory crossover understands the practice as involving the transfer of models.[7] I briefly review this literature to show why the case of evolutionary theory does not fit this picture and an alternative account is needed.

Well-studied cases include the Ising model, which was developed to describe ferromagnetism and found its way into social science to model phenomena as diverse as urban segregation and stock market behavior (Knuuttila & Loettgers, 2014; 2016; Yee, 2021); the Lotka–Volterra equations, which are widely applied to describe and explain such diverse phenomena as predator–prey interactions in biology, economic growth cycles, and the spread of technological innovations (Knuuttila & Loettgers, 2017; Houkes & Zwart, 2019; Humphreys, 2019; Herfeld, 2025); the Yule process, which was developed in biology to describe birth and speciation processes with constant birth/speciation rates, and is now used

---

[5] Other authors (e.g., Campbell, 1965; Hodgson, 2009; Lewens, 2015; Schulz, 2020) have presented different typologies of how evolutionary theory impacts non-biological areas of research. These were not intended as taxonomies of the *general* phenomenon of crossover of evolutionary thinking into other fields, though, but restricted to evolutionary social science, evolutionary economics, and cultural evolution.

[6] Whether a scientific theory as a whole could even travel between fields depends on what theories are. I cannot pursue this issue here, but see French (2020), Winther (2021), or Frigg (2023) for excellent entry points into the debate on the nature of scientific theories.

[7] Literature can be found under various keywords, including "physics transfer" (Boumans, 1993), "knowledge transfer" (Herfeld & Lisciandra, 2019; Humphreys, 2019; Boumans, 2023), "model transfer" (Knuuttila & Loettgers, 2020; Tieleman, 2022; Lenhard & Hasse, 2023; Herfeld, 2025), or "template transfer" (Houkes & Zwart, 2019; Houkes, 2023; Humphreys & Lin, 2023). Grüne-Yanoff & Mäki (2014) call it "model exchange" and argue that it is a unitary kind of interdisciplinarity that can be covered by an overarching philosophical account.

to describe the growth rates of firms of different sizes (Tieleman, 2022); and econophysics, a field that emerged in the 1990s through attempts to use models from statistical physics to explain economic phenomena, in particular in the area of finance (Rickles, 2007; Kuhlmann, 2019; Yee, 2021). But why would a model of ferromagnetism adequately describe stock markets, and why would a model of birth and speciation processes adequately describe and explain the growth of firms?

The models involved in such cases are a specific type of scientific models, namely, as Frigg (2023) calls them, nonmaterial models. These can for instance be verbal descriptions of a phenomenon or of the behavior of a system, but in cases of model transfer they usually are formal models (for a detailed discussion of these different kinds of models, see Frigg, 2023: 394, 404ff.). Think for example of a system of differential equations, which specifies a structure of relations between the variables that describe relevant features of a system – such as Maxwell's equations, which can be found in most physics textbooks as a set of coupled partial differential equations ready to be applied in practice. In their source fields, formal models usually have ontological interpretations that are provided by the broader theoretical context, that is, a mapping of their variables and the relations between them onto salient aspects of the systems or phenomena covered by the theory. The assumption here is that the ways in which the model's variables relate to each other faithfully represents the ways in which the system's parts affect each other, or in which the phenomenon's parameters covary. In this way, models typically are embedded in the ontology of their source field.[8]

Transferring a model into a target field then involves detaching it from its original ontological interpretation and developing an ontological reinterpretation for the target domain, that is, a remapping of the model's variables and relations between them onto salient aspects of the phenomena studied in the target domain. An early analysis of this procedure was given by Mayntz (1992: 65–67; 1997a: 316; 1997b: 307–308), who calls it "generalization and respecification" (Mayntz, 1997a: 316; my translation). The first step, generalization, turns the components taken from the source domain into generally applicable templates by breaking the connection with the source domain's ontology. The second step, respecification,

---

[8] Note that in the relevant literature no particular philosophical view is assumed of what kind of ontology (an object ontology, a process ontology, and so on) would be preferred. Here, too, with "ontology" I simply mean an inventory of the relevant kinds of entities (objects, processes, substances, etc.), properties, relations, and so on that are recognized in a particular domain of study.

forges connections between a template and the specific ontology of the target domain. Mayntz (1992: 30) holds that for generalization and respecification to be successful, the ontologies of the source and target domains cannot be too different. This is easy to see: since in both the source and target field a mapping of the model's variables and relations onto the field's ontology takes place, this can only be done if the respective ontologies are not widely divergent (cf. Knuuttila & Loettgers, 2016; Reydon, 2021: 82–84). In other words, successful model transfer requires an ontological basis.

In the literature on model transfer, this is often seen as justification of transfer on the basis of drawing an analogy between the systems under consideration (for discussion, see for example Frigg, 2023: 289ff.; Herfeld, 2025). But I contend (see Section 1.2) that only very strong analogies can support model transfers that have explanatory and predictive force – analogies that do not merely highlight *some* important similarities between two systems or processes, but that show how these can be seen as two different instances of the same general process or system. For example, Kuhlmann (2019) suggests that the ontological basis enables the formulation of mechanistic explanations that in both cases explain phenomena by highlighting the same general mechanism of behaviors of the systems' parts and of interactions between them. With respect to the examples mentioned earlier, when abstracting away from their material realizations, ferromagnets and stock markets, and populations and firms, allegedly possess the same general structure of entities with specific behaviors and interactions between them, such that they instantiate the same abstract kind of mechanism. The question whether and why such an approach would work thus is primarily an ontological question, namely whether the general, abstract structures of the systems or phenomena that are examined in the source and target domains – the kinds of entities involved in the respective mechanisms, and their behaviors and interactions – are the same such that they can be considered instances of the same general system or phenomenon. (Whether or not this should still count as drawing analogies is a question I am happy to leave open.)

The general picture that emerges is as follows. The application of a theory in a new domain requires the availability in the source domain of a (set of) model(s) – usual formal models – that describe the general category of phenomena covered by the theory and that can be abstracted and reinterpreted for application in the target domain. The conceptual and ontological embedding of the formal model in the source domain can guide the procedure of generalization and reinterpretation: the ontological interpretation of a model in its source domain can guide researchers as to what kinds of entities and interactions to look for in the target domain as potential applications of the model that is in focus. This is a promising account of how crossovers generally occur. Applying evolutionary theory in a new field would thus involve choosing the most suitable model of the evolutionary process from the available set of models of evolution, checking whether the ontological criteria for transfer are met, and abstracting and reinterpreting the model in a suitable way for the case at hand.

While in practice this will often be easier said than done, in what follows I will argue that this account faces a deeper-lying problem. This problem is that transferrable models of the evolutionary process *per se*, that is, abstract descriptions of the evolutionary processes as a whole, are unavailable. Models of many specific subprocesses are available for transfer, but no general model of the evolutionary process *as such*. This is because of the pluralism inherent in evolutionary theorizing with respect to the processes and phenomena it accounts for and the causal factors that it invokes (see Section 3). Evolution just is not a neat general process that can be captured by models the transfer of which into new fields would make these into evolutionary fields in any meaningful way – evolution is too complex a phenomenon for that.

2.2 The Conditions for Natural Selection Are Not a General Model of Evolution

Evolutionary biologists study a staggeringly large variety of systems that evolve in very different ways: microbes are very different beings from oaks, and neither are very similar to slime molds or gorillas, to name some random organisms. Populations of microbes, oaks, slime molds, and gorillas exhibit quite different evolutionary dynamics and, accordingly, evolutionary theorizing has always been thoroughly pluralistic regarding the explanatory factors that can be cited to explain evolutionary phenomena. While evolutionary biologists generally recognize four principal causes of evolutionary change (natural selection, genetic drift, mutation, and migration), not all of these are always invoked to explain evolutionary phenomena and several other causal factors often play important roles too. Richard Lewontin (1991: 461) put it aptly: "evolutionary theory [...] is a collection of descriptions of mechanisms connected with each other by the life cycle of organisms and which are of greater and lesser relevance in different cases."

Concrete instances of evolution can involve different combinations of processes, none of which necessarily occurs in every instance. To be sure, there are certain necessary requirements for evolution to occur (evolutionary processes need at least a population of reproducing or replicating entities that exhibit some heritable variation).[9] But my claim is that there is no *general process* of evolution in the sense that there is no unique set of causal factors that operate in all instances of the evolutionary process – there is no essence of evolution. Accordingly, there is no general description of *the* evolutionary process, that is, no model *of evolution* that would be transferrable between fields in applications of evolutionary theory outside biology.

Many readers will balk at this claim (and several have) and respond that there *is* an essence to evolution – namely some version of the triplet "variation-reproduction-selection." Godfrey-Smith (2009: 17) understands formulations of this type as attempts at providing "an abstract summary of what is essential to the process" of evolution by natural selection. According to Godfrey-Smith, they "give a *summary* of the evolutionary process in the form of a *recipe* for change" (2009: 18–19; original italics) that "tend to have three ingredients: variation, heredity, and differences in reproductive output" (2009: 19). Indeed, as I will discuss in Section 4, this triplet is widely used in crossovers of evolutionary theory into other fields. But I believe it is not correct to understand the triplet as a summary of the evolutionary process.

The triplet view is usually traced back to Lewontin's (1970) famous formulation of three conditions for the occurrence of natural selection. According to Lewontin (1970: 1), the principle of evolution by natural selection encompasses three sub-principles: individuals in a population must vary phenotypically (variation), different phenotypes must survive and reproduce at different rates in a given environment (differential fitness), and parents and offspring must correlate with respect to their contribution to the next generation (fitness is heritable). Lewontin emphasizes the generality of these principles: not only biological populations but any population of entities for which these three principles hold will undergo evolution by natural selection. He asserts that

> [t]hese three principles embody the principle of evolution by natural selection. While they hold, a population will undergo evolutionary change. [...] The generality of the principles of natural selection means that any entities in nature that have variation, reproduction, and heritability may evolve. (Lewontin, 1970: 1)

---

[9] Compare Godfrey-Smith's (2009) notion of "Darwinian populations" as the entities that have the capacity to undergo evolution by natural selection. I discuss this in Section 4.3.

It is important to see that Lewontin's set of principles, which he calls "Darwin's scheme," is not a model of the dynamics of natural selection, but a specification of the *conditions under which* natural selection can and will occur. Lewontin specifies that it is the "logical skeleton" (1970: 1) of Darwin's argument in Chapter 4 of the *Origin of Species* for the claim that natural selection occurs in nature. As the skeleton of that argument, "Darwin's scheme" specifies necessary and sufficient conditions for natural selection to occur and Darwin's argument in the *Origin* amounts to showing that these conditions are met.

But a specification of necessary and sufficient conditions for a process to occur is not a description of the dynamics of the process or a recipe that tells us how the process should occur to yield the desired result. "Darwin's scheme" is too unspecific – too flattened – a description of natural selection to provide a causal or mechanistic explanation of the evolutionary process of change. As a bare-bones argument for the occurrence of natural selection it provides a good starting point for adequate explanations, but it isn't itself an explanatory model.

Moreover, even if "Darwin's scheme" were an explanatory model of natural selection, it would still not be a model *of evolution*. This is a second way in which triplet formulations constitute severely flattened accounts of evolution. Lewontin (1991) saw clearly that evolution is much richer than the process of natural selection. Natural selection is only one of the explanatory principles that are commonly invoked in evolutionary explanations in biology, such that taking Lewontin's "Darwin's scheme" or a similar three-part scheme as representing evolution amounts to a strongly flattened account that obscures the richness of evolutionary processes that occur in nature. Lewontin himself raised this criticism against selectionist approaches in cultural evolution, clarifying that the three-part scheme only represents *one form* of evolution (Fracchia & Lewontin, 1999; 2005).[10] And elsewhere, he pointed out that the explanatory force of "Darwin's scheme" is very limited: "The trouble with this outline is that it does not explain the actual forms of life that have evolved. There is an immense amount of biology that is missing." (Lewontin, 2010).

But doesn't the full title of Darwin's *Origin of Species* specify that evolution proceeds "by means of natural selection," indicating that the

---

[10] Equating evolution with natural selection, Fracchia & Lewontin (2005: 17) state, is found in "the writings of vulgarizing enthusiasts who have simplified evolutionary biology in a way that seriously misleads"!

process of natural selection constitutes the core of biological evolutionary theory such that crossovers should hinge on models of selection? While selection indeed tends to play an important role in the three modes of crossover that I distinguish in Section 4, the matter isn't that simple. From Darwin's work onward, evolutionary theorizing encompassed heated debates on the importance of natural selection as explanatory factor. Darwin's work initiated a lineage of approaches that involve natural selection, but also a variety of responses in the form of alternative theories of evolution that often de-emphasize selection as a causal factor in evolution and sometimes explicitly deny selection a role (Bowler, 1983; 2005; 2017; Depew & Weber, 1995; Levit et al., 2008). Biologists of Darwin's time were largely convinced *that* evolution – understood as the transformation of organismal forms through time – occurred, but diverged greatly on *how* it occurred and, most importantly, what its underlying causes were. As Romanes (1892: 12) put it, "[t]here is a great distinction to be drawn between the fact of evolution and the manner of it."

The debates on "the manner of it" continue to the present day (see Section 3). These concern the precise content of evolutionary theory, that is, the questions what exactly are its core principles, its fundamental assumptions about the causes of evolution, its explanatory structure, the centrality of natural selection as explanans, and more. In particular, controversies pertain to the relative importance of the various causes of evolution (Beatty, 1986). In the more than 160 years that passed since the publication of Darwin's *Origin*, evolutionary theorizing has not settled on a definitive account of how evolution works. Indeed, the differences between the stages of evolutionary theorizing are so large that one may legitimately wonder to what extent these can still be conceived of as developments of *the same theory* (cf. Hull, 1988; French, 2020: 149). This lack of agreement on the theory's core principles and assumptions make it difficult to conceive of evolutionary theory as available in the form of models that all satisfy the theory's core principles and assumptions.

In particular, evolution without selection commonly occurs (most prominently through genetic drift) and, conversely, natural selection depends on other factors to cause adaptive evolutionary change, such that selection is neither a necessary nor a sufficient ingredient of evolutionary explanations (Section 3; Reydon, 2023). But even when considering natural selection as the core of evolution, no unified account is available (see Pence, 2021: 3–4, 9, 15–16; Ruse, 2023). The nature of natural selection, and the questions what and how natural selection explains, are ongoing issues in the philosophy of biology (Reydon, 2023; Gildenhuys, 2024). One question here is whether natural selection is actually a *cause* of evolutionary change or rather merely the *statistical outcome* of evolutionary change that is driven by other causes (Walsh et al., 2002; 2017; see Pence, 2021; Ruse, 2023: 132–135) – and if it is a cause, whether it is best understood as a force (Sober, 1984; Luque, 2016), or a mechanism (Skipper & Millstein, 2005). Different views on this issue entail different views of the position of natural selection in evolutionary theory and of how it explains biological phenomena.

A related debate concerns the question *what* selection explains. Here at least two different issues are in focus. The first is the innovative potential of natural selection, that is, the question whether natural selection explains the emergence of novel traits or only their spreading through a lineage once they have emerged; the issue is often phrased as the question whether selection explains the "*arrival* of the fittest" or merely their *survival* once they have arrived (Reydon, 2011; McLoone, 2022). The second involves the question whether natural selection explains the *actual traits* of individual organisms, or only *trait distributions* in populations. Proponents of the so-called "Negative View" of selection hold the latter view (Stegmann, 2010; Birch, 2012; McLoone, 2022).

The existence of such debates may seem surprising, as evolutionary theory's long history of success and its central role in biological science would be reasons to expect that biologists would have resolved such issues long ago. But it is precisely the enormous diversity of evolving systems that biologists study that makes these issues unresolvable: some cases support one answer, other cases other answers. The precise content of these debates is less relevant for the topic of this Element, though. For my purposes it suffices to note that evolutionary theory never became stabilized in the way many other scientific theories have, namely by reaching a generally agreed-upon, unified formulation of its explananda, its explanatory principles, and its ontology. Biologists and philosophers of biology keep disagreeing over what, exactly, evolutionary theory explains, how it explains, and what kinds of entities and causal factors occupy center stage. Because of this, evolutionary theory lacks general models that can be thought of as describing the general category of evolutionary processes *as such*, or the essence of evolution, and could serve as templates facilitating theory travel in the way discussed earlier.

To be sure, formalisms *do* play key roles in evolutionary research, and mathematical models are widely used. For instance, the Lotka–Volterra equations, mentioned earlier, cover competitive interactions between species, such as predator–prey and host–parasite dynamics. Similarly, the Price Equation, another key model in evolutionary biology, covers frequency changes of alleles or traits in populations subject to selection and transmission between generations, and is an important tool to distinguish between the contributions of these two factors to population dynamics (Gardner, 2020). But these formalisms do not represent *the* evolutionary process or the general behavior of all evolving systems, and as such cannot be thought of as transferrable models *of evolution*. They describe specific aspects of evolution or specific subprocesses that can occur within a much richer evolutionary process. While applying the Lotka–Volterra equations to economic growth cycles amounts to transferring *some* explanatory content from evolutionary biology, that by itself doesn't mean that economic growth cycles can be understood as evolutionary phenomena in any meaningful way. *A fortiori*, such applications fall far short of making fields of research into evolutionary fields of research in the full sense of the term.

The same holds for the Price Equation. It models population dynamics in terms of trait or allele frequency changes while distinguishing between a selective and a nonselective component of change (Gardner, 2020; Lewens, 2024: 32ff.). While this is an important aspect of biological evolution, biological evolution encompasses an incredibly diverse set of processes, explananda, and explanatory factors, most of which the equation does not cover. The Price equation describes one phenomenon that can be observed in many evolving populations, but not the evolutionary process itself. Applying the Price equation outside biology thus can hardly be thought of as applying evolutionary theory or transferring a model *of evolution* from biology to another field.

And the same holds for cultural evolution. As Fogarty et al. (2024) explain, the mathematical models that occupy center stage in cultural evolution are based on models from population genetics: "The foundations of much modern cultural evolutionary theory can be traced directly to models and methods from population genetics, which formed a baseline from which a theory of the transmission and evolution of cultural traits could be developed. The relationship between the two disciplines runs deep" (Fogarty et al., 2024: 2). But population genetics does not equal evolution – it is an important part of evolutionary theory, but the latter is much richer than population genetics, in particular with respect to the explanatory factors that are recognized.

To make the points from this section more concisely, I first sketch the pluralism inherent in evolutionary theory with respect to both its explananda and the explanatory factors it invokes to explain them (Section 3). While biologists and philosophers of biology have long recognized that biological evolution is a process that occurs in a large variety of ways and that evolutionary theory is a rich, disunified, pluralistic theory (Mayr, 1985; Dupré, 2003: 12–26), this pluralism remains insufficiently recognized in crossover attempts, resulting in, as argued earlier, flattened descriptions of evolution being applied in crossovers. Accordingly, Section 3 is intended to showcase the richness of biological evolutionary theorizing and how much of this richness such flattened descriptions miss, that is, how much unused potential for crossover there is. In addition, it is intended to show that even in biology a common core of causal factors that feature in all evolutionary explanations is lacking (even though evolutionary explanations have a common *structure* – see Reydon, 2023). This supports my claim that evolution is too complex a phenomenon to be capturable in a ready-for-use model the transfer of which would render a field evolutionary in a meaningful way. In Section 4 I then examine the principal modes of crossover to show that these indeed involve flattened accounts of evolution.

3 The Source Field: Evolutionary Theorizing in Biology

3.1 Darwin's Theory

The *Origin* presented a theory that was devised to explain a specific set of phenomena in a specific domain of investigation. In the book's introduction, Darwin (1859: 1–4) mentions the explananda: the geographical distribution of kinds of organisms and their geological succession at the same location; the clustered diversity of organismal forms (the existence of groups of highly similar organisms, that is, the "origin of species") and the mutual affinities between clusters; the admirable "perfection of structure and coadaptation" and the "coadaptations of organic beings to each other and their physical conditions of life." With respect to coadaptation, Darwin later clarifies that he does not only mean adaptation of organisms to their environments (i.e., to local conditions of existence, including other organisms), but also the mutual *internal* adaptedness of the different parts of the organism: "all those exquisite adaptations of one part of the organization to another part, and to the conditions of life, and of one distinct organic being to another being" (Darwin, 1859: 60).

Darwin highlights two principal factors – common descent and natural selection – to explain these phenomena, presenting these as specifications of the underlying nature of two "great laws" that were already widely accepted by biologists of his time:

> It is generally acknowledged that all organic beings have been formed on two great laws – Unity of Type, and the Conditions of Existence. By unity of type is meant that fundamental agreement in structure, which we see in organic beings of the same class, and which is quite independent of their habits of life. On my theory, *unity of type is explained by unity of descent*. The expression of *conditions of existence* [...] *is fully embraced by the principle of natural selection*. [... But] the law of the Conditions of Existence is the higher law; as it includes, through the inheritance of former adaptations, that of Unity of Type. (Darwin, 1859: 206; emphasis added)

This quotation suggests a minimal explanatory structure for Darwin's theory: the principal explananda are two distinct phenomena, namely the occurrence of similar structures and traits in organisms of the same group (fundamental agreement in structure and traits in organic beings of the same group *independent of their habits of life*), and the adaptedness of organisms to their abiotic and biotic environments (which is where the habits of life in relation to the conditions of existence come into play); structural and trait similarities are explained by common descent, adaptedness by natural selection.

Here a principal aspect of the divergence between biological evolutionary theorizing and instances of crossover already becomes visible. As I will explain in Section 4, the explanatory structure used in crossovers of evolutionary theory typically is even more minimalistic than this minimal explanatory structure: often common descent is lacking. Moreover, Darwin's theory is considerably more complicated and pluralistic than this minimal explanatory structure.

One issue is the connection between Darwin's two explanatory factors. Darwin calls natural selection the "higher law," because when explaining unity of type common descent presupposes selection (Huneman, 2017: 85). This is because the presence of an adaptive trait in a contemporary group of organisms cannot be explained by invoking natural selection as acting only when the trait arose in early ancestors of the group, after which the trait was passed on from ancestors to present-day organisms through common descent. Natural selection often also plays a role in the retention of the trait in the lineage from early ancestors to the present: producing traits is costly for the organism, so a novel trait must continue to be selectively favored to remain present in the lineage (stabilizing selection). For many traits, unity of type (structural and trait similarity) thus is explained as a consequence of common descent under the assumption that natural selection continues to operate – common descent alone cannot explain it. In this sense, natural selection often has *explanatory* priority over common descent.

In addition, natural selection has *causal* priority, because on Darwin's view selection drives the branching of lineages, that is, speciation, by causing diverging adaptations to manifest themselves in a population ("divergence of character"), eventually causing splits into specialized populations (disruptive selection; Darwin, 1859: 111–129; Sober, 2009). In this sense, common descent is a product of selection.

But common descent is not less important than natural selection, nor is natural selection the sole explanatory factor. Darwin considered common descent a real cause of evolutionary phenomena for the existence of which there is good evidence, thus acknowledging its own explanatory power next to natural selection (Reydon, 2023). Indeed, early adopters of Darwin's theory held widely diverging beliefs regarding the explanatory factors underlying evolution and while not all accepted natural selection, there was wide agreement on common descent as such a factor (Mayr, 1985; Depew & Weber, 1995: 2; McLoone, 2022). But note that while natural selection and common descent are *logically* independent (McLoone, 2022), they are materially interdependent. Natural selection cannot produce adaptations without common descent of the members of an evolving population. Adaptive traits and structures are slowly carved out by selection in a gradual, multi-generation process occurring in lineages of organisms connected by common descent. While natural selection is one of the causes of lineage formation, the existence of lineages is a prerequisite for natural selection to produce adaptations. In addition, common descent has *evidential* priority, as traits due to selection are not necessarily good evidence for common descent (because they can arise independently on multiple occasions due to similar selection pressures), whereas traits *not* due to selection *can* serve as such (Darwin, 1859: 427; Sober 2009; but see Ruse, 2023: 86–90). Natural selection and common descent thus each address their own explananda (adaptedness and similarity, respectively), but nonetheless depend on each other to explain them.

Moreover, as we saw, similarity and adaptedness are only two explananda, and Darwin mentions others: the geographical distribution of organismal forms, their succession through geological time at one location, the affinities between kinds of organisms (i.e., the obvious similarities in traits and structures between species), and the "perfection of structure." This latter phenomenon – the machine-like, functional, complex organization of organisms, that is, the mutual internal adaptedness of the different parts of the organism mentioned above – has been in focus throughout the history of evolutionary theorizing since well before Darwin (Ågren, 2021: 20). William Paley highlighted it in his 1802 book, *Natural Theology* (and Darwin is often thought to have been motivated by reading some of Paley's work as a student at Cambridge).

Notably, most of these explananda (or parallel explananda) are not in view in the fields into which evolutionary theorizing crosses. As will be shown in Section 4, the explananda typically in view in crossovers of evolutionary theory are diversity of forms of the entities under study (but much less the mutual affinity between clusters of similar entities, that is, the relations of descent between "species" of entities) and in particular the adaptedness of entities to external conditions (but much less their *internal* adaptedness).

Note, too, that Darwin considered natural selection and descent insufficient to explain all these explananda, or even just diversity/similarity and adaptedness. To explain them, Darwin is thoroughly pluralistic regarding explanatory factors. At the end of the *Origin*, Darwin's explanatory pluralism clearly surfaces when he summarizes his theory:

> these elaborately constructed forms [...] have all been produced by laws acting around us. These laws, taken in the largest sense, being Growth with Reproduction; Inheritance which is almost implied by reproduction; Variability from the indirect and direct action of the external conditions of life, and from use and disuse; a Ratio of Increase so high as to lead to a Struggle for Life, and as a consequence to Natural Selection, entailing Divergence of Character and Extinction of less-improved forms. (Darwin, 1859: 489–490)

Darwin here mentions several "laws," which he discusses throughout the *Origin*, often emphasizing how little they were known: laws of growth (general principles governing organismal development), laws governing reproduction, laws of inheritance, laws governing the production of variation, and Malthus's law (that populations increase at larger rates than the rates of increase in resources – itself a case of crossover from economics into biology).[11] Not mentioned in the above quotation are the laws governing correlation of growth ("the whole organization is so tied together during its growth and development, that when slight variations in any one part occur, and are accumulated through natural selection, other parts

---

[11] Even though Darwin does not use the term "population," Darwin was inspired by Malthus' work and conceived of evolution in terms of populations of organisms.

become modified" – Darwin, 1859: 143), the laws of hybrid sterility, to which Darwin devotes considerable space in Chapter VIII of the *Origin* (as hybrid sterility is an important factor enabling separate evolution of closely related lineages), and sexual selection (which Darwin takes as an important cause of many traits and for which he distinguishes two types, male-to-male combat for available mates and female mate choice).

Darwin treats these laws as separate explanatory factors. For example, in several locations in the *Origin* Darwin (1859: 143ff., 466) discusses laws of correlation of growth, emphasizing "the importance of the laws of correlation in modifying important structures, *independently of utility and, therefore, of natural selection*" (Darwin, 1859: 144; emphasis added). This is not to say that Darwin treats all factors as equal: natural selection is primary, but it cannot explain all aspects of evolutionary change. Moreover, it cannot perform its explanatory work all by itself. In the first edition of the *Origin*, Darwin remarks: "I am convinced that Natural Selection has been the main but not exclusive means of modification" (Darwin, 1859: 6). He repeats this remark more emphatically in later editions and elsewhere even expresses his feeling that he may have placed too much emphasis on natural selection as a cause of evolution (Hoquet, 2018: 5; see also Delisle & Tierney, 2022: 138, who go as far as to argue that natural selection is *not* the explanatory core of Darwin's theory; for discussion, see Ruse, 2023: 86–90).

It is important to note that Darwin's own theory is difficult to pin down due to his prolific writing and constant revision of already published work. Two famous essays preceding the *Origin* already presented the theory of evolution by natural selection (Darwin, 1909). In particular the essay of 1844 contains a very detailed presentation, which however differs considerably from the theory in the *Origin*: whereas for instance the 1844 version describes evolution as occurring in episodes of destabilization of a species with natural selection only operating until stabilization sets in again, in the 1859 version evolution and natural selection occur continuously (Partridge, 2018).[12] The *Origin* itself was published in six sometimes considerably revised editions, and in later editions Darwin more strongly highlighted the role of causal factors other than natural selection (Liepman, 1981). And the *Origin* "was literally only an abstract of the manuscript Darwin had originally intended [...] as the formal presentation of his views on evolution" (Stauffer, 1975: 1). Darwin initially

---

[12] Partridge (2018) gives a detailed comparison of the two versions, suggesting that they are radically different. White et al. (2021: 102) consider them moderately different.

planned to publish a much larger book titled *Natural Selection* that would present his complete theory. He used two chapters of the manuscript as the basis for his 1868 two-volume *The Variation of Animals and Plants under Domestication*, but the larger manuscript was only published a century after the sixth, final edition of the *Origin* (Stauffer, 1975).

Which text, if any, represents the definitive, or most consistent, or best elaborated version of the theory – the "real Darwin"? Historians' and philosophers' attempts to answer this question through detailed studies of the extensive volume of Darwin's published and unpublished writings did not yield a "real Darwin," but a deeply pluralist picture of Darwin's thinking. Hoquet (2018), for example, provides a detailed discussion of the various interpretations of Darwin's work and argues that these are irreducible to a single, definitive version of Darwin's theory. Even in Darwin's work the relative importance of the various causes of evolution remains an unsettled issue.

3.2 Neo-Darwinism and Orthogenesis

The second half of the nineteenth century saw an intense debate on Darwin's principle of natural selection that led to the emergence of an ultra-selectionist camp and an anti-selectionist camp. Many biologists doubted that there was sufficient evidence to claim that many organismal traits were adaptive, and thus doubted the explanatory power of natural selection (Bowler, 1983: 3ff.). Even some of Darwin's close allies expressed reservations (Mayr, 1985). The result was what Julian Huxley (1942: 22) called "the eclipse of Darwinism" and a promulgation of alternatives to the Darwinian view.[13]

One such alternative, orthogenesis, shows how the debate was foremost about the comparative importance of explanatory factors. Proponents of orthogenesis prioritized the laws of growth (which Darwin recognized but considered unknown) over natural selection in explanations of organismal forms: because the laws controlling organismal development determine which organismal forms and traits are possible in the first place, they channel evolutionary processes in the direction of possible forms. Many orthogeneticists flat-out rejected Darwin's theory. Others, however, saw evolution as adaptive and acknowledged natural selection as a causal factor, while considering laws of growth as dominant (Bowler, 1983: 155, 167–171).

---

[13] Bowler (1983) discusses the debates and alternative accounts. Romanes (1892: Chapter IX) provides a first-hand overview of the criticisms of Darwin's view by a participant in the debates. On orthogenesis, see Bowler (1983: 141ff.), Levit & Olsson (2006), or Levit et al. (2008).

On the ultra-selectionist side, a shift away from Darwin's views occurred in Neo-Darwinism, a version of Darwin's theory that was promoted by Alfred Russel Wallace and August Weismann, and that differs from Darwin's theory in important respects. Darwin held (following Lamarck) that trait changes during an organism's lifetime, for example due to changes in its environment, could be passed on to offspring. Weismann rejected such inheritance of acquired traits and singled out natural selection as *the* cause of evolutionary change, seeing his view as going "beyond Darwin's conclusions" (Weissmann, 1893: 338; cf. Bowler, 2005). Wallace similarly emphasized natural selection as by far the dominant – if not only – causal factor in evolution. In his exposition of his views, notably published under the title *Darwinism*, Wallace (1889: viii) emphasizes his "differences from some of Darwin's views" and claims to "take up Darwin's earlier position, from which he somewhat receded in the later editions of his works" (*ibid.*). This "pure Darwinism," as Wallace (1889: viii) perceived his own view, emphasizes "the overwhelming importance of Natural Selection *over all other agencies* in the production of new species" (Wallace, 1889: vii; emphasis added).

Romanes (1895: 12) characterized this view as "the pure theory of natural selection to the exclusion of any supplementary theory," with natural selection as "the sole means of modification, excepting in the case of Man" (Romanes, 1895: 6). He (Romanes, 1895: 1–12) provides an illuminating overview of the most important differences between Darwin's theory and Neo-Darwinism, harshly criticizing the latter as having "misunderstood the teachings of Darwin" (Romanes, 1895: 11) and even to "hide certain parts of Darwin's teaching, and give undue prominence to others" (Romanes, 1895: 9). Neither Weissman nor Wallace, however, claims that natural selection is the sole causal factor operating in evolutionary processes – they only strongly foreground natural selection as dominant in evolutionary processes.

Here another aspect of the divergence between biological evolutionary theorizing and instances of crossover is visible. While many contemporary cases of crossover involve strongly selectionist views of evolution and as such connect to late nineteenth-century ultra-selectionism (Sections 4.2 and 4.3), in contrast current developments in evolutionary theorizing see a return of laws of organismal development as well as an appreciation for inheritance of acquired traits, albeit not in their nineteenth-century versions (see Section 3.5).

3.3 The Modern Synthesis

A third major stage in evolutionary theorizing is the Modern Synthesis in the 1930–1940s. It is not a scientific theory but rather a historical epoch in which several hitherto largely separate branches of biology, including genetics, systematics, and paleontology, were "bound together [...] into a unified and progressive science" (Smocovitis, 1992: 3; 1996; cf. Mayr, 1980: 40–41). Julian Huxley, who coined the name "Modern Synthesis," writes that:

> [b]iology in the last twenty years [...] has embarked upon a period of synthesis, until to-day it no longer presents the spectacle of a number of semi-independent and largely contradictory sub-sciences [...] As one chief result, there has been a rebirth of Darwinism. (Huxley, 1942: 26).

Indeed, the Modern Synthesis to a large extent reversed the "eclipse of Darwinism" by again emphasizing Darwin's ideas about evolution, without however returning to Darwin's theory. Through the synthesis of previously disconnected parts of biology, the Modern Synthesis achieved a much richer and more encompassing account of the living world than any predecessor. But it should be noted that the Modern Synthesis did not converge on a single, orthodox theory of evolution, but rather encompassed some variety of viewpoints regarding how evolution occurs. Indeed, while some of the architects of the Modern Synthesis entertained considerably more pluralistic views of evolution than others, the Modern Synthesis became less pluralistic as it settled (Beatty, 1986). Yet, the connections that were forged changed both the explanandum and the explanans in evolutionary theorizing, such that the Modern Synthesis version differs in important respects from its predecessors (e.g., Smocovitis, 1992; 1996; Delisle, 2017; Delisle & Tierney, 2022).

Perhaps most importantly, the connection between Darwin's theory and genetics paved the way for a shift toward describing and explaining evolutionary change at the molecular rather than organismal level. Darwin's theory lacked an adequate account of the basis of variation between organisms and Darwin held a deeply mistaken view of inheritance. The way to better accounts only opened up with the rediscovery of Mendel's work in 1900 and the development of statistical population genetics in the 1920–1930s. Danish botanist Wilhelm Johannsen introduced the term "gene" in 1909 to denote the – at the time purely theoretical – heritable units that co-determine the properties of developing organisms, insisting that the new term was completely neutral with respect to the nature of these units, their mechanism of inheritance and the way in which they co-determine organismal traits. For him the term was "a short and unprejudiced word for unit-factors" (Johannsen, 1923: 136). This allowed researchers to use Mendelian genetics to study population-level changes before the material basis of genes had been uncovered (Falk, 2009: 158ff.). It also brought genetic mutation, genetic drift within populations, and gene flow between populations (due to migration and outcrossing) into play as important causal factors in evolution. Where Darwin mentions a manifold of unknown laws of variation and development and describes variation at the level of organismal traits, the Modern Synthesis could now offer a novel explanation of the nature of variation and development in terms of genes, even though the material nature of genes was not yet understood (Bowler, 2005).

This fundamentally changed the explanatory structure of evolutionary theory. For Darwin and the Neo-Darwinists, the principal entities in the evolutionary process were organisms and their traits in the context of organism-level competition. This picture of evolution hinges on Darwin's notion of a "struggle for life" or "struggle for existence," which results from Malthus's law:

> as more individuals are produced than can possibly survive, there must in every case be a struggle for existence, either one individual with another of the same species, or with the individuals of a distinct species, or with the physical conditions of life (Darwin, 1859: 63).

This struggle encompasses competition between organisms for resources and struggles of organisms with their environments, and is a struggle for both survival and reproductive success. Malthus's law explains the occurrence of struggles for existence, which in turn explains the occurrence of natural selection, which in turn explains divergence of character (the occurrence of new traits and organismal forms) and extinction.

Darwin explains that he uses the term "struggle" "in a large and metaphorical sense" (Darwin, 1859: 62), referring to "not only the life of the individual, but success in leaving progeny" (*ibid.*) and encompassing competition as well as mutual dependencies between organisms. He gives examples of two animals actually struggling with each other for food, a plant struggling against drought, and a parasitic mistletoe being dependent on the tree on which it grows and struggling with the tree "only in a far-fetched sense" (Darwin, 1859: 63). Darwin (1859: 77–79, 314, 350, 396, 408, 477) repeatedly mentions the relations between organisms as driving evolutionary change, even suggesting that these are more important than organism–environment relations: "the most important of all causes of organic change is one which is almost independent of altered and perhaps suddenly altered physical conditions, namely, the mutual relation of organism to organism" (Darwin, 1859: 487).

Organisms are the protagonists in this explanatory sequence, a sequence that cannot be realized on the Modern Synthesis view of evolution.

The integration of genetics into the Modern Synthesis caused a shift of focus from organismal traits to the "unit-factors" underlying them, leading to what some authors consider a multi-faceted "eclipse of organisms" (Huneman, 2010: 366; Nicholson, 2014; Baedke, 2025) and a view of evolution with genes as protagonists. And *evolution itself is understood differently*: while for Darwin evolution is the differential survival and reproduction of organismal forms, for the Modern Synthesis evolution is the change of gene frequencies in populations. Populations – the entities that evolve – are understood differently too: ontologically, they are gene pools rather than groups of breeding and otherwise interacting organisms (as they were for Darwin).

Accordingly, in the Modern Synthesis, the struggle for existence moves out of sight (Lewens, 2010; Walsh, 2010: 321; 2012: 201) and with it Malthus's law. Natural selection is no longer explained as ensuing from organisms' struggle for existence, but from differential replication of competing genes. And natural selection explains changes in gene frequencies in populations over time, only indirectly accounting for the explananda that Darwin had in view. Indeed, in this sense the notion of natural selection in the Modern Synthesis is not the same as in Darwin's theory (Lewens, 2010). This ontological shift is clearly visible in Huxley's summary of the Modern Synthesis view of evolution: "Natural selection, acting on the heritable variation provided by the mutations and recombination of a Mendelian genetic constitution, is the main agency of biological evolution."[14] Organism-level struggles are not even mentioned. As "[t]he theory of Darwinian evolution was reduced to that of changes in gene (allele) frequencies" (Falk, 2009: 159), the laws of organismal growth receded into the background too.

3.4 The Gene's-Eye View and the Neutral Theory

The second half of the twentieth century saw two major developments in evolutionary theorizing that shifted the perspective even further away from the organismal to the molecular level: the Gene's-Eye View and the Neutral Theory.

The Gene's-Eye View is associated with George C. Williams' 1966 book, *Adaptation and Natural Selection*, and Dawkins 1976 bestseller, *The Selfish Gene*, but can be traced back to the origins of the Modern Synthesis (Ågren, 2021: 27). A key aspect is the fundamental understanding of evolution in

---

[14] Letter from Julian Huxley to Ernst Mayr, 3 September 1951 (quoted in Huneman, 2017: 77).

terms of competition not *between organisms* but *between genes* (or more precisely, between alleles at the same chromosomal location in different organisms – Ågren, 2021: 67), "striving" (in a metaphorical sense) to leave as many copies of themselves as possible in the next generation. Genes rather than organisms are the beneficiaries of natural selection (i.e., the entities that succeed with respect to survival and reproduction/replication in instances of selection) and the relevant selective environment is the gene's, not the organism's (Ågren, 2021: 52–53, 61).

But organisms still have *some* role in the Gene's-Eye View, albeit more peripherally. Dawkins famously distinguishes between "replicators" and "vehicles": genes are replicators, entities of which the structure is faithfully replicated into the next generation, whereas organisms merely are the containers (vehicles) that carry these replicators. The metaphorical "striving" of genes to leave as many copies of themselves as possible is what drives evolution, while organisms are merely means to this end. On the Gene's-Eye View, evolution thus is the differential replication of replicators in competition with other replicators, where competition is mediated by organisms who interact with their environment and with each other.

While Dawkins calls this organism-level interaction "vehicle selection," vehicle selection is different from selection at the organism level for Darwin: while Darwin focused on organisms differing in *their* reproductive success, for Dawkins "[v]ehicle selection is the process by which some vehicles are more successful than other vehicles in ensuring the survival of their replicators" (Dawkins, 1982: 46). Because in sexual reproduction offspring do not carry exactly the same alleles as their parents, reproductive success at the organism level in terms of number of offspring is usually not the same as success regarding the spread of an organism's alleles. Accordingly, for Dawkins replicators, not vehicles, are the beneficiaries of selection, such that adaptation should be explained at the genetic level. Only replicators have explanatory import (Wilkins & Bourrat, 2022).[15]

Note that in crossovers of evolutionary theory researchers often somewhat loosely invoke the replicator–interactor framework, which however is different from Dawkins' replicator–vehicle framework in an important respect. Hull (1980; 1981) coined the term "interactor" instead of Dawkins' "vehicle" to emphasize the causal and thus explanatory role

---

[15] For Dawkins, vehicles are found at all organizational levels (e.g., chromosomes, cells, multispecies groups, or even ecosystems) except the genetic level. Replicators only occur at the genetic level, but besides genes any part of an organism's genome up to the entire genome can in principle be a replicator. Compare this view to Mayr's, quoted below, on which only whole genomes are subjects of selection.

of organisms as mediators between genes and the selective environment: interactors are "entities which produce differential replication by means of directly interacting as cohesive wholes with their environments" (Hull, 1981: 33). Where Dawkins locates causality and thus explanatory importance with replicators, Hull's framework is more ecumenical in attributing organisms a causal and explanatory role as well. Crossovers of evolutionary theory that build on the Gene's-Eye View thus should specify which version is used (and some indeed do: Hodgson & Knudsen, 2010: 165ff.; Section 4.3).

Some authors consider the gene-centrism immanent in the Gene's-Eye View to be an intrinsic part of the Modern Synthesis (Walsh, 2010; Pigliucci & Müller, 2010: 14). But not all of the major figures in the Modern Synthesis did in fact accept gene-centrism (Ågren, 2021: 189). Mayr, for instance, expresses his view of evolution in strong terminology:

> An individual either survives or doesn't, an individual either reproduces or doesn't, an individual either reproduces very successfully or it doesn't. The idea that a few people have about the gene being the target of selection is completely impractical; a gene is never visible to natural selection, and in the genotype, it is always in the context with other genes, and the interaction with those other genes make a particular gene either more favorable or less favorable. [...] In the 30's and 40's, it was widely accepted that genes were the target of selection, because that was the only way they could be made accessible to mathematics, but now we know that it is really the whole genotype of the individual, not the gene. [...] Dawkins' basic theory of the gene being the object of evolution *is totally non-Darwinian*.[16]

If anything, this quotation shows how even the most prominent advocated of Darwinian evolutionary theory disagree on what Darwinian evolution encompasses.

The history sketched so far is one of a changing and diminishing role of organisms in evolution. What changed was which entities are seen as the *beneficiaries* of selection and which as *causally driving* evolution. For Darwin and nineteenth-century Neo-Darwinism, evolution was driven by the organism-level struggle for existence and thus centered on the organism's success in surviving and reproducing. Organisms lost this central position to some extent in the Modern Synthesis, and further receded into the background in the Gene's-Eye View as genes took over as the beneficiaries of selection and drivers of evolution.

---

[16] Ernst Mayr: *What Evolution Is* (interview in *Edge*, www.edge.org/3rd_culture/mayr/mayr_index.html; emphasis added).

A similar focus on the genetic level is embodied in the "Neutral Theory of Molecular Evolution" (Kimura, 1968; 1983; King & Jukes, 1969). It also sees evolution from a molecular viewpoint, but in contrast to the strongly selectionist Gene's-Eye View, the Neutral Theory emphasizes selectively neutral genetic mutations as the drivers of evolution. Some proponents present the Neutral Theory as being non-Darwinian (King & Jukes, 1969). However, the Neutral Theory does not reject natural selection but merely attributes it a less central role, emphasizing the importance of non-Darwinian molecular evolution (genetic drift) over natural selection occurring at the organism level. The Neutral Theory thus is not non-Darwinian, but merely considers drift much more important than selection (Depew & Weber, 1995: 362–363). While some recent authors claim that "the neutral theory has been overwhelmingly rejected" (Kern & Hahn, 2018: 1369), others respond that "it is now abundantly clear that the foundational ideas presented five decades ago [in the neutral theory] are indeed correct" (Jensen et al., 2019: 111). The debate continues.

The Gene's-Eye View and the Neutral Theory reduce evolution to gene frequency changes due to competition between alleles, and drift, respectively, further sidelining the plurality of explanatory factors recognized by Darwin, many Neo-Darwinists and the Modern Synthesis. But the latest development in evolutionary theorizing has the pendulum swinging back to an increasingly pluralistic view.

3.5 An Extended Synthesis?

As the most recent stage of Darwinian thinking, the Extended (Evolutionary) Synthesis is conceived of as a revision and extension of the Modern Synthesis that adds explanatory factors to the explanatory framework already in place (Pigliucci & Müller, 2010; Laland et al., 2015). The Extended Synthesis still is in the making: there is a controversial debate on the question whether such a revision is needed at all, and if so, what exactly it should look like (Laland et al., 2014; Huneman & Walsh, 2017; Lewens, 2019; Lala et al., 2024). At present, competing frameworks are still being developed and it is difficult to assess what the explanatory core and ontological commitments of an Extended Synthesis will turn out to be.

One important aspect of the debate concerns the question whether the available theory misses important causal factors in evolution such that additional explanatory elements should be brought into play to fill lacunae in the explanatory structure of the theory (Laland et al., 2014; Aaby et al., 2024) – and if so, which factors should be added. Prominent candidates are nongenetic inheritance, niche construction, phenotypic plasticity, and developmental constraints (Baedke et al., 2020). According to proponents of an Extended Synthesis, such additions would change the nature of the theory, perhaps in drastic ways, and entail a radically different view of how evolutionary processes occur. For instance, Jablonka & Lamb (2005; 2020) have long argued that nongenetic inheritance mechanisms should be incorporated into evolutionary theory, such as epigenetic (via non-DNA-caused changes in gene expression),[17] behavioral (imitation-based) and symbolic inheritance. This would not only yield a fundamentally revised view of inheritance, moving away from the gene-centrism of the Gene's-Eye View and from a conceptualization of evolution as changes in gene frequencies. Proponents of an Extended Synthesis hold that it also would entail a fundamentally different view of the origins of variation in populations and reintroduce the possibility of Lamarckian inheritance of acquired traits (Laland et al., 2015; Jablonka & Lamb, 2005; 2020). Indeed, biologists are increasingly arguing that evolution encompasses some Lamarckian elements (Koonin & Wolf, 2009; Burkhardt, 2013).

Another feature is a twofold role of organisms as causal factors in evolution. Niche construction theory (Odling-Smee et al., 2003; Laland et al., 2015: 4–5; Lala et al., 2024: 113–115), for example, emphasizes that organisms are not struggling for existence in a pre-given, fixed environment, but rather actively co-create their selective environments: many animals build structures such as nests, webs, or beaver dams, plants actively change soil nutrient cycles and the composition of the soil microbiome, and so on. Organisms thus are not passive subjects of environmental selection pressures but to some extent can bias selection by changing their selective environment.

In addition, organismal developmental mechanisms have come into focus as factors that can bias the direction of evolution (Walsh, 2010; Love, 2024). Organismal development relies on robust growth processes with a limited spectrum of viable outcomes, limiting the trajectories available for evolution by natural selection to take. If a particular organismal structure is not physically or chemically viable, or there is no feasible developmental trajectory to realize it, it is an evolutionary nonstarter. Accordingly, biologists have long emphasized the role of organismal development – the laws of growth – as posing constraints on the directions evolution can take (Gould, 1977; Alberch, 1980; Maynard Smith et al., 1985), but differed on the

---

[17] For an overview, see Lacal & Ventura (2018).

question exactly how restrictive these constraints were (with orthogenesis as an extreme position seeing constraints as so restrictive as to dominate evolutionary processes). Proponents of an Extended Synthesis not only acknowledge a constraining role of development, but argue that organismal development also can bias the direction of evolution through developmental plasticity (Lala et al., 2024; Nicoglou, 2024). This is the capacity of organisms to change parts of their phenotype during development in response to environmental circumstances (West-Eberhard, 2003: 34ff.), which enables organisms to colonize new environments, contributes to the production of variation, and sometimes increases the chances of speciation (Laland et al., 2015: 3). Plasticity thus *opens up* trajectories for evolution, rather than merely constraining them, and as such can be a driving factor in evolution.

Here we find another iteration of the debate on the relative importance of natural selection – this time not about the *overall* importance of natural selection as a cause of evolution, but about the question under which conditions selection is the principal causal factor in an evolutionary process and in what cases other factors dominate. A central thesis in thinking about an Extended Synthesis is that organisms should come into focus as potential causes of directionality in evolution that can bias the direction of evolution by modifying their phenotypes or their selective environments. Depending on the strength of phenotypic plasticity and niche construction, these factors may have more explanatory import than natural selection regarding the products of evolution, but the relative importance of these factors will differ per case.

While the content of a possible Extended Synthesis remains to be determined and divergent views are debated among its proponents (Lewens, 2019), it seems clear that it will be strongly pluralistic. It encompasses a return of organisms as causal agents in evolution (Huneman, 2010; Laland et al., 2014; Nicholson, 2014; Baedke, 2025), entailing a strongly pluralistic conception of what evolution *is* that (at least according to proponents of an Extended Synthesis) goes well beyond the Modern Synthesis conception of evolution as changes in gene frequencies in populations *and* beyond Darwin's view of evolution as the differential survival and reproduction of organisms of different forms (see Love, 2019: 318).

3.6 Taking Stock

Recall Romanes' remark that "[t]here is a great distinction to be drawn between the fact of evolution and the manner of it" (1892: 12). The preceding discussion showed that not only is there persistent disagreement regarding the "manner of it," but more importantly there even *is* no unique "manner of it." Evolution is not a unique process that is instantiated in the same way in various material systems, but rather one that occurs in different ways in different cases, with different causal factors taking center stage. Furthermore, evolutionary theorizing has always been aimed at explaining a variety of phenomena of life (cf. Delisle & Tierney, 2022: 49ff.). This is why evolutionary theorizing is concerned with "a collection of descriptions of mechanisms [...] which are of greater and lesser relevance in different cases" (Lewontin, 1991: 461; quoted earlier), and the history of theorizing swings between strong explanatory pluralism that treats multiple causes on a par in explanations of the phenomena of life, and views that emphasize natural selection as the principal explanatory factor.

The preceding Sections 3.1–3.5 can be condensed into two tables that showcase part of the pluralism inherent in evolutionary theorizing – but note that with these I do not aim to provide a complete list of the explananda and explanantia of evolutionary theorizing. Table 1 lists eight principal explananda. These do not constitute a single category of phenomena and, more importantly, natural selection isn't always the principal

Table 1 The principal phenomena of life explained by evolutionary thinking.

Level of organization or domain of investigation	Phenomenon to be explained
Organism	Complex functional structures (inner functionality of the organism as a system of interacting components, adaptedness of parts of the organism to each other); Adaptedness of organisms to external conditions of existence
Population	Changes in gene (allele) frequencies over time; Changes in organismal trait frequencies over time
Narrower geographical location	Diachronic succession of forms (species) in the same geographical location
Wider geographical location/whole planet	Geographical distribution of kinds of organisms (of organismal forms and traits)
Taxonomy	Clustered diversity (kinds of organismal forms/species); Relations between clusters with similar traits (species)

factor in their explanation or, for that matter, even always part of the explanation. Table 2 lists the principal explanatory factors.

Regarding crossovers of evolutionary theory into other fields, the preceding review highlights two important issues. First, the source field on which self-identifying "evolutionary" fields and approaches draw cannot be understood as containing a single, currently best version of evolutionary theory that would be susceptible to model transfer. Accordingly, crossovers should not be understood as cases in which evolutionary theory is simply applied to a category of non-biological phenomena or models of the evolutionary process are used to model non-biological phenomena.

The second issue is particularly salient with respect to two modes of crossover (Sections 4.2 and 4.3): natural selection doesn't operate by itself, and organismal traits and structures are never explained by natural selection alone, but by combinations of factors. This insight counts against views that strongly emphasize natural selection. Ironically, in crossovers discussed in Sections 4.2 and 4.3, researchers typically employ strongly flattened accounts of evolution that almost exclusively focus on selection and ignore the actual richness and pluralism of biological evolutionary theorizing. This circumstance does not necessarily affect their research practices in a negative way and it does provide opportunities to develop

Table 2 The principal explanantia in evolutionary thinking.

Level of organization or domain of investigation	Explanatory factor
Gene/genome	Natural selection of alleles; Common descent of alleles; Genetic drift
Organism	Struggle for life (competition and cooperation); Natural selection of organisms; Common descent of organisms; Sexual selection; Migration; Laws of growth/development, correlations of growth; Niche construction; Phenotypic plasticity
Group	Natural selection of groups; Common descent of groups; Niche construction?

novel approaches in the target fields. But it does raise questions about the nature and strength of the *explanations* that are being devised in those fields (if they are aimed at explaining phenomena, which is not always the case). It cannot be expected that taking a one causal factor from biological evolutionary theory – one that is deeply connected to other factors, as was shown above – will yield evolutionary explanations or even an evolutionary approach in any meaningful sense.

I will now discuss the principal modes of crossover and in the final section explain how these *can* meaningfully be understood as yielding evolutionary fields and approaches.

4 Three Modes of Crossover

4.1 Evolution as Natural History: Bridging Fields

The currently most widespread mode of crossover of epistemic content from biology into other fields is what I call the *Natural History Mode*. It involves the use of knowledge about the evolutionary history of specific kinds of living beings to establish bridges between evolutionary biology and otherwise nonevolutionary domains of investigation. The strategy is to understand products of evolution by way of their origins, that is, to achieve a better understanding of the nature of particular organismal traits through highlighting causal aspects of the evolutionary trajectories in which they arose. Even though this strategy can in principle be applied throughout the living world, typically in focus in non-biological domains of investigation are human cognitive and behavioral traits – that is, *human nature*.

This mode of crossover traces back at least to Darwin's 1871 seminal work, *The Descent of Man*, in which among other things he attempted to explain such phenomena as human sociability, cooperativeness, and morality as products of the species' evolutionary history (Reydon, 2015; Desmond et al., 2024). Darwin speaks of a "moral sense" as a principal distinction between humans and other animals that originated in social instincts, that is, human intuitions, emotions, feelings of sympathy, and so on (Allhoff, 2003). On Darwin's view, sociability, cooperativeness, and other such traits arose in ancestral species as instinctive responses to particular situations and became widespread through processes of natural and sexual selection. Such responses can become widespread in an ancestor lineage if they provide selective advantages to the groups of which these organisms were members (i.e., due to group-level selection), Darwin suggested, subsequently become part of human innate behavioral tendencies, and much later (after the arrival of language) become codified as behavioral and moral rules. Accordingly, knowledge about the evolutionary history of the moral sense is crucial for understanding the nature of human morality.

Several fields outside biology have followed Darwin's lead in looking at human natural history to explain human behavior and mental traits, including evolutionary ethics, evolutionary psychology, evolutionary anthropology, evolutionary economics, and evolutionary sociology.

Contemporary evolutionary ethics looks at human natural history to elucidate the evolutionary foundations of morality (for a history and overview of the field, see Allhoff, 2003; Clavien, 2015; Ruse & Richards, 2017).[18] An important question here pertains to the evolution of altruism. In biology, altruism is not an ethical but rather a purely behavioral phenomenon consisting of cases "where an animal behaves in such a way as to promote the advantages of other members of the species not its direct descendants at the expense of its own" (Hamilton, 1963: 354). Biological altruism thus is behavior that enhances the survival and reproduction of other organisms at a cost to the survival and/or reproductive success of the organism exhibiting the behavior. The connection with morality is made by the assumption that morality is codified altruistic behavior in humans, which as a product of human evolutionary history would be at least in part innate and not completely due to upbringing, education and social environment. The various accounts of the evolutionary origins of altruism only provide indirect evidence for such innateness claims, however: they only show that under certain conditions it is *possible* for altruistic behavior to arise in evolution, not that it *in fact* is a product of our species' evolutionary history.

Assuming behavior to be a product of natural selection and organisms to be the principal beneficiaries of selection, the occurrence of altruism constitutes a problem because altruistic behavior reduces the fitness of the organism exhibiting the behavior while benefiting others: the altruist supports others in their efforts at survival and reproduction and as a consequence can invest less in its own survival and reproduction. How could such behavior have been selected and become widespread? Various

---

[18] Not all authors explore the evolutionary basis of morality in a positive sense. Since the early 2000s so-called *evolutionary debunking arguments* have begun to appear that say that moral beliefs are unlikely to track any moral truths, because moral beliefs are merely those that proved adaptive in human evolutionary history. Vavova (2015) provides an introduction to the topic. More recently, evolutionary debunking arguments have also been applied to other realist positions besides moral realism.

solutions to this problem have been proposed that latch onto different levels of biological organization to show that altruistic behavior can in principle arise and become widespread due to natural selection (Nowak, 2006b; Godfrey-Smith, 2009: 115–121).

Group selection is one important type of approach, introduced by Darwin in *The Descent of Man* (Sober & Wilson, 1998; Wilson, 2002; Borello, 2005). While Darwin's theory of evolution is fundamentally organism-centered in the sense that the organismal "struggle for life" drives evolutionary processes and organisms are the principal beneficiaries of selection, Darwin acknowledges that organisms are not necessarily the sole beneficiaries of selection in terms of fitness and not the only entities that can be engaged in a "struggle for life" – groups can be too. But group selection remains subject to ongoing controversy among biologists.

Persistent questions are whether a concept of group selection is necessary to explain phenomena such as altruism (as usually adequate organism-level explanations are available), whether groups are indeed the kind of things that can be subject to selection (as groups don't reproduce in the way organisms do, and usually lack the organizational integrity to interact with their environments as wholes), and how the concept of group selection should be understood in the first place (Okasha, 2001; 2006; Ågren, 2021: 35–45). Today, the controversy has become part of a broader debate on the levels of selection and multi-level selection theory, which understands natural selection as being able to operate on multiple levels simultaneously, including the gene, organism, and group levels. Despite this controversy, group selection remains an important approach in evolutionary accounts of human morality and sociality (Sober & Wilson, 1998; Wilson, 2002).

Another approach, *kin selection* (see Rubin, 2024), highlights the fact that because of the genetic similarity between closely related organisms, helping one's kin reproduce contributes indirectly to the spread of some of one's own genes. Here, the focus is on genes rather than organisms or groups: from a genetic point of view altruism can arise when the cost incurred by the altruist from a particular behavior is below a specific threshold and there is a sufficient degree of relatedness between the altruist and the beneficiary ("Hamilton's Rule" – Hamilton, 1963; Ågren, 2021: 116ff.).

As this approach only covers altruistic behavior between sufficiently closely related organisms, Trivers (1971) introduced the model of *reciprocal altruism* to explain the occurrence of altruism between organisms more generally. In this model, organisms typically reciprocate behavior, such that altruism does not come at a cost to the altruist (and probably should not count as altruism in any strong sense). Trivers' model focuses on the organism level and shows how altruistic behavior can spread in a population where selection operates against organisms that do not reciprocate altruistic acts they receive, leaving reciprocating organisms with a selective advantage.

The discussion on the correct explanation of biological altruism continues today. What these approaches show, though, is that behavior that we would interpret as altruistic – and hence as morally relevant – can *in principle* arise in evolutionary processes, such that morality *may* have an evolutionary basis.

Altruism is merely one aspect of human nature, however. In his famous – and controversial – 1975 book, *Sociobiology: The New Synthesis*, entomologist E. O. Wilson laid out the groundwork for an integrative biological science of social behavior that shares the general motivation of evolutionary ethics but has a much broader scope. Most of the book deals with the evolutionary basis of behavior in species other than humans. The first and last chapters, however, explicitly formulate the aim of "biologizing" (Wilson's terminology) the social sciences by "reformulat[ing] the foundations of the social sciences in a way that draws these subjects into the Modern Synthesis" (Wilson, 1975: 4), such that "the humanities and social sciences shrink to specialized branches of biology [...] and anthropology and sociology together constitute the sociobiology of a single primate species" (Wilson, 1975: 547). The scope of the research program includes the "biologizing" of ethics by explaining moral behaviors – as well as the lack thereof – by reference to fitness advantages (Wilson, 1975: 562–564).

In a later paper, Wilson and Ruse specify the aim as transforming ethics into an applied science on the assumption that "[m]oral premises relate only to our physical nature and are the result of an idiosyncratic genetic history" and "morality rests ultimately on sentiments and feelings" (Ruse & Wilson, 1986: 173, 190).[19] Understandably, such claims caused considerable controversy regarding a number of issues, including the worry that sociobiology assumed human behaviors to be genetically determined and therefore resistant to change through social, political, or educational measures (see Lewontin, 1980, for the criticism and Kurzban & Haselton, 2006: 159–151, for a defense; for in-depth discussions of the controversies, see Kitcher, 1985; Segerstråle, 2000).

In writings published four decades later, the scope of the research program remains as broad as it was from the start. A volume coedited by Wilson and titled *Darwin's Bridge* (Carroll et al., 2016) aims at uniting the

---

[19] Note the connection to Darwin's view, discussed earlier.

humanities and the sciences using human evolutionary history as a bridge between disciplines. It includes chapters on the evolutionary basis of such diverse aspects of human culture as bullying and free-riding, morality, literature, mark-making, and personality traits and narrative identity. Wilson describes the overarching aim of the program as to "explain [...] *why* we possess our special nature and not some other out of a vast number conceivable" (Wilson, 2016: 3; original emphasis) and mentions the causal role of selection at various levels of biological organization (multilevel selection) as one of the program's fundamental assumptions.

Sociobiology's approach to investigating human behavior and the human mind is continued today by several contemporary fields that self-identify as "evolutionary," including evolutionary psychology, evolutionary anthropology, evolutionary aesthetics, and evolutionary sociology (which are not strictly separate fields but overlap to some extent – Barkow, 2006: 5–6). The general phenomenon in focus is human nature, that is, the set of innate behaviors, proclivities, ways of thinking and feeling, and so on, that is so widespread in the human population that it can be thought of as a defining characteristic of humans. Human nature manifests itself not only in social behavior but also in worldviews, morality, language, science, the creation of art, and so on, hence the development of multiple fields that each focus on their own aspect of human nature. The explanantia in these fields consist of historical accounts that specify how certain ways of behavior and certain inclinations (such as curiosity about nature, or the desire to paint or to play an instrument) were selectively advantageous to individuals or to their groups in earlier stages of the evolution of the human lineage, either in the context of sexual selection in early humans or in the context of natural selection in earlier lineages leading up to humans.

The fundamental assumption underlying these fields is that the evolutionary history of the human species provides information regarding what kind of beings we are. The assumption that human behavioral and mental traits were produced by selection is an auxiliary assumption that plays an important role in many approaches but strictly speaking is not essential for any of the abovementioned fields. For example, Barkow (2006: 40–41) explains that the adaptationist perspective in evolutionary psychology often only functions as a "metanarrative" – a general framework that helps evolutionary psychologists make sense of human behavior and cognition – and as a "heuristic stance" that helps researchers generate hypotheses about the biological basis of human nature. Other such heuristic stances are possible, however, such as a more pluralistic evolutionary perspective that invokes a variety of evolutionary factors besides natural selection, such as genetic drift or developmental constraints (cf. Kurzban & Haselton, 2006: 153–154).

At first sight, the fundamental assumption is not implausible: humans are products of evolution in the same way as all other living beings are, so we may reasonably expect evolutionary history to provide *some* information about the nature of our species (Hamilton, 1963). However, a key question is *how much* and *what exactly* the evolutionary history that ultimately led to modern humans can tell us about who and what we are. Let me illustrate this issue by taking a closer look at the role of the concept of human nature in reasoning in the abovementioned fields.

The epistemic content that is transferred from biology into the various "evolutionary" fields mentioned earlier does not consist of models (or other descriptions) of the dynamics of evolution, and in particular not of models that represent one of the specific views of evolution discussed in Section 3, but rather of historical facts about the descent of *Homo sapiens*. This claim may sound surprising, as group selection and reciprocal altruism are studied on the basis of mathematical models and computer simulations. But besides the fact that these models are not models of evolution as such (in the same way as the Lotka–Volterra equations or the Price equation are not models *of evolution* – see Section 2.2), it is important to see that these models are not transferred from biology into evolutionary ethics and other fields. What is transferred are the *results* of modeling exercises in biology that show how *biological* altruism can arise, and that evolutionary ethicists then interpret as having specific implications for *ethical* altruism. The models themselves remain in their home field.

Elsewhere (Reydon, 2015), I have argued that such crossovers involve the notion of human nature as a *bridge concept* and that crossover of epistemic content occurs in two steps, which I called the "argument to human nature" and the "argument from human nature." These occur not only in evolutionary ethics, evolutionary sociology, and other such fields, but also more broadly in political, social and economic thought (Reydon, 2015; for economics, see Schulz, 2020: 95–162). The argument *to* human nature encompasses the biological search for the evolutionary basis of widespread human behavioral and cognitive traits. The argument *from* human nature uses the account of human nature that was obtained in the first step as a basis for making ethical, political, and social claims. The notion of human nature serves as a hinge between these two steps, which both face difficulties.

The argument to human nature is problematic, because evolutionary theory in fact says less about human nature and human societies than we often think it does, as philosophers have long argued (Dupré, 2000; 2001; 2003; Midgley, 2002; Ruse, 2017). Dupré (2001: 75–76), for example, points out that there is no general reason to assume that an entity's origins convey important information about its nature. In the specific case of biological evolution, the mere fact *that* a trait has evolved does not necessarily provide much information about its nature (Dupré, 2003: 96). This is because all organismal traits have an evolutionary history but all are also due to the organism's development in its specific environment, and it typically is difficult to discern which causal factors – history or environment, or "nature or nurture" – are dominant in the explanation of a trait.

Consider cooperativeness in humans. Many people are inclined to cooperate with others, but there also are many who are not so inclined. Have humans been molded by natural selection to be cooperative and is a lack of cooperativeness an aberration to be explained by the circumstances in which someone grew up, or is it precisely the other way around? Or are both ends of the spectrum and all the different degrees of (lack of) cooperativeness in between them equally attributable to selection? Are they products of selection at all? And *if* we could be certain that cooperativeness is due to natural selection, what were the relevant selection pressures? What is required to answer such questions is detailed information about the circumstances under which the trait evolved in ancestral populations and under which it became widespread and changed further in later stages of evolution – information which usually is lacking. Therefore, rather than speculating about the evolutionary origins of behavior, perhaps we might learn much more about human behavior by systematically observing actual human behavior as it manifests itself in present-day humans under known conditions (Dupré, 2003: 97; Ramsey, 2023).[20]

Yet speculation about human evolutionary history remains an important part of some approaches. For instance, some evolutionary psychologists assume that the human mind is fundamentally adapted to life in small hunter-gatherer groups in the Pleistocene – circumstances very

---

[20] Interestingly, evolutionary economics provides a case that supports this suggestion. Hodgson (2019: 34–39) argues that group selection theory supports the claim that humans are at least to some extent cooperative and thus refutes the core assumption of neoclassical economics that humans are self-interested utility maximizers. But this reasoning seems incorrect: while group selection theory only tells us that human cooperativeness *can* be a product of selection, much stronger evidence for human cooperativeness can be achieved from empirical studies of actual human behavior in the here and now. Moreover, neoclassical economics understands self-interestedness merely as acting according to one's own preferences, which can include preferences for altruistic actions, such that group selection theory could not refute the core assumption.

different from present-day life in cities and global food supply chains. What they call the "Environment of Evolutionary Adaptedness" (Tooby & Cosmides, 1990) is not a concrete selective environment at a particular location and time on Earth, but rather the general conditions that are assumed to have obtained throughout the Pleistocene. But it is doubtful whether these general conditions constitute sufficiently specific knowledge regarding the circumstances under which the human mind actually evolved to draw inferences regarding the nature of human mental and behavioral traits. Why assume that conditions in the Pleistocene remained sufficiently unchanging to count as a stable selective environment?

Moreover, even though the Pleistocene was the principal era during which modern humans evolved, this doesn't mean that by far most of the evolution of the human mind occurred during the Pleistocene rather than before and/or after (Dupré, 2003: 80–81; Buller, 2005). The Pleistocene assumption along with other key assumptions in evolutionary psychology (for instance regarding the speed of evolutionary processes) have accordingly drawn a considerable amount of criticism from philosophers of science (Dupré, 2001; 2003; Buller, 2005; Smith, 2020). These criticisms highlight that such auxiliary assumptions generally are very difficult to support, such that inferences about human nature from human natural history must remain speculative. In part due to these issues, the concept of human nature itself has come under renewed scrutiny (Buller, 2005; Hannon & Lewens, 2018; Ramsey, 2023).

In addition to the problem of determining the selective environment in which human nature evolved, there is the problem of identifying relevant traits that may be innate to humans. To do so, researchers rely on comparative analyses that involve searching for trait similarities in closely related species (Mazur, 1978; Reydon 2015; 2023; Schulz, 2020: 95–129). If a particular trait is widespread in humans and also found in more rudimentary forms in one or several closely related primate species, this suggests that the trait may have evolved in a common ancestor and thus probably is innate in humans (Mazur, 1978). However, it still remains possible that the trait arose independently in *Homo sapiens* and in related species, and was propagated in humans by social learning. Ultimately, then, claims that a trait is part of human nature to some extent must remain tentative (Gould, 1976; Dupré, 2003; Reydon, 2015).

Additional problems occur in the argument from human nature. *Even if* it were possible to establish beyond reasonable doubt that a particular behavioral or mental trait is innate, it is unclear what this would mean for our broader understanding of that trait, as the notion of innateness can be understood in numerous ways (Mameli & Bateson, 2006). This is an issue with profound practical consequences, as scholars have long strived to use knowledge about human nature as a basis for political views and social measures (Reydon, 2015). A contemporary proponent is biologist David Sloan Wilson (2007; 2011; 2019), who has long been promoting evolutionary thinking as a broad worldview to ground the improvement of politics, cities, societies, and human life more generally. But for attempts to use human nature as a basis for devising policies and for interventions to succeed, we must be able to assess how biological knowledge about human nature would relate to our contemporary lives.

Consider for example the possible implications of knowledge about the evolutionary history of human nature for general well-being. While the starting assumption of evolutionary psychology is merely *that* human mental and behavioral traits supervene on a physiological basis that is a product of evolution (James, 1890), to make evolutionary history informative about human well-being auxiliary assumptions are required. The "evolutionary mismatch hypothesis," for instance, rests on the Pleistocene assumption and states that many human traits and behaviors are adapted to living circumstances in the Pleistocene that no longer obtain today, such that many problems with well-being in contemporary humans can be understood as mismatches between the circumstances to which behavior and the mind have adapted and the circumstances in which contemporary humans find themselves (Li et al., 2018). Many evolutionary psychologists and Darwinian psychiatrists (McGuire & Troisi, 1998) accordingly ask how human nature *detracts* from well-being. This hypothesis also plays a role in some approaches in evolutionary medicine (Williams & Nesse, 1991; Nesse & Williams, 1994), for instance in claims that conditions such as obesity and diabetes are due to a mismatch between the nutritionally dire circumstances to which our metabolic system has adapted in our ancestors and the contemporary overabundance of high-calorie foods (Gluckman & Hanson, 2006).[21] Other authors, in contrast, such as proponents of so-called "positive (evolutionary) psychology" (Geher et al., 2023; Larsen & Witoszek, 2024), attempt to identify aspects of human nature that are positively associated with well-being, and ask how we can actively foster these.

---

[21] Even though evolutionary medicine does not use the concept of human nature (as human nature is typically understood as referring to innate behavioral and mental traits), some approaches in the field use the same strategy by using human natural history to obtain knowledge about the physiological systems in the human body, and identify mismatches between earlier adaptations and contemporary lifestyles.

But how can we decide between these divergent interpretations? The mere fact *that* a trait is a product of adaptation to ancestral living circumstances doesn't usually help us decide whether it constitutes a mismatch with current circumstances, or is positively connected to human well-being, or is neutral in this respect, because by far most traits occur in modern humans various manifestations and diverging degrees. Having a thirst for freedom may be a human universal, as Larsen & Witoszek (2024: 10–24) claim, but people have different degrees of desire for freedom and sometimes strongly diverging ideas of what freedom is. Some people desire absolute freedom to do as they like, whereas others want to be free to follow strong political or religious leaders. Is either of these an evolutionary mismatch or rather an aspect of the human mind that is positively connected to well-being? Are such desires best understood as adaptations at all, or is their evolutionary history much less important than cultural factors? Finding the correct interpretation seems impossible without very detailed historical knowledge about the circumstances under which our desire for freedom evolved over millions of years.

Note that not all self-proclaimed evolutionary fields that employ the Natural History Mode of crossover use human nature as a bridge concept and thus can avoid the problems connected to this concept. Evolutionary history (Russell, 2003; 2011), for instance, does not revolve around human nature, but examines how biological evolution affected human history and *vice versa*. As such, it can be thought of as a subfield of environmental history, the field that studies how events and trajectories in human history have been affected by local and global environmental circumstances (Diamond, 1997) and, conversely, how human presence has changed local environments (Isenberg, 2014). Indeed, this is not only a topic for historians, but for ethicists too: it is a central pillar of Aldo Leopold's "land ethic" (Leopold, 1949: 205–207; Millstein, 2024) and thus could play a role in evolutionary ethics understood broadly as including evolutionary approaches to environmental ethics.

Evolutionary history adds an explicitly evolutionary perspective to this interplay between human environments and human history. It emphasizes how human practices have affected the evolution of local nonhuman populations (hunting African elephants for ivory drove elephant populations toward increasing tusklessness: Russell, 2011: 17–25), how human-induced evolution has shaped human history (the Industrial Revolution was only possible because of the availability of specific breeds of cotton that had been bred by indigenous populations in the New World for 5,000 years: Russell, 2011: 103–131), and how human populations and populations of other species at the same location coevolved (lactose tolerance coevolved in humans with increasing milk production in cattle: Russell, 2011: 91–94). Evolutionary history thus connects knowledge about human natural history with knowledge about nonhuman natural history, but without invoking human nature to bridge these.

The preceding discussions show that the Natural History Mode of crossover essentially consists in using knowledge about the natural history of our species to achieve knowledge about typical human traits. (Note, though, that this mode is not exclusive to what may be called the evolutionary human sciences, but is also sometimes found elsewhere, such as in evolutionary veterinary science and medicine – see LeGrand & Brown, 2002; Veit & Browning, 2023.) This is a mode of crossover of evolutionary theory into other fields, but only in a weak sense, as what the theory says about the dynamics of evolution features as *background to the natural history knowledge* that is used. Natural selection and common descent (and sometimes other factors such as genetic drift) are commonly invoked as part of the explanations that are provided, but feature there as background assumptions regarding the way human evolution occurred and are not used to describe and explain the dynamics of concrete evolutionary processes. The interest is foremost in establishing *that* certain human traits are products of evolution (under the assumption that evolution involves natural selection and common descent), and then in establishing what that fact would mean for human life and the image we have of ourselves.

With respect to this second interest natural selection is assumed as the basis for evaluative claims about specific traits, that is, claims about the kind of beings humans are and how our kind of being (mis)matches our current ways of living. Schulz (2020: 15ff.) points out that in evolutionary economics this way of reasoning also serves to provide evidence for claims regarding how human decision-making occurs. In this respect invoking natural selection is a crucial part of the reasoning in the evolutionary human sciences insofar as these aim for such evaluative and evidential claims. Common descent is invoked in comparative analyses of related species, but the explanatory role of descent in combination with selection in Darwin's theory does not usually play a role. While some authors conceive of this practice as a reduction of the study of humans to subfields of biology (most prominently: Wilson, 1975), I believe this is much too strong an interpretation of what is encompassed in the Natural History Mode, as the specific causes of evolutionary processes are considered less important. Accordingly, the Natural History Mode does not connect specifically to one of the stages of evolutionary theorizing discussed in Section 3, but rather only takes a strongly flattened view of evolution (one that only encompasses the concepts of natural selection and common descent) as a background assumption.

4.2 Evolution as an Algorithm: Exploring Design Spaces

What I call the *Algorithmic Mode* of crossover rests on the conception of biological evolutionary processes as involving specific implementations of a general, abstract algorithm that can be implemented in a broad array of natural and artificial systems. It underpins fields such as evolutionary computing, evolutionary robotics, and evolutionary electronics, that are concerned with a specific kind of problems. These are problems that do not have only one or a limited set of correct solutions, but a – sometimes extremely – large number of potential solutions. These potential solutions encompass tradeoffs between different parameters, some performing better on some parameters while others perform better on other parameters, while all being sufficiently good solutions to the problem at hand. The relevant parameters thus span up a huge "solution space" or "design space" in which some areas contain good solutions but large areas do not contain feasible options. The task is to search the space for those patches where sufficiently workable solutions are found.

The problems in view here are *design tasks*: think of designing robots able to navigate difficult terrain, writing software for a particular application, designing electronic circuits, optimizing factory assembly processes, or finding pharmaceutically functional macromolecules among thousands of candidate molecular structures (Mitchell & Taylor, 1999; Bredeche, 2015; Eiben & Smith, 2015; Winfield, 2024). Characteristic for many desired solutions is that these should not only be *adaptive*, that is, well fitted to the particular function that has been specified, but also *adaptable*, that is, sufficiently changeable to continue to perform that function when conditions change (Mitchell & Taylor, 1999: 593). Whether the product is a robot, a software script, or a drug, designers and companies usually want to be able to easily update a product in light of new demands rather than having to redesign them or even design new products from scratch. But once a particular design has been chosen, this limits which areas of the design space are accessible for future modifications, as these have to be built on the basis of the existing design.

This latches onto two key aspects of natural selection. Because of the sheer size of the search space, systematic searches for the best or even very good solutions is not a task that human engineers and designers can perform well (Miikulainen & Forrest, 2021: 9). The guiding assumption of this mode of crossover is that this is exactly what natural selection does in biology: "[e]volution is [...] a method of searching among an enormous number of possibilities – e.g., the set of possible gene sequences – for 'solutions' that allow organisms to survive and reproduce in their environments" (Mitchell & Taylor, 1999: 593). In addition, the desideratum of finding solutions that are not only adaptive but also adaptable is realized by natural selection. Evolution occurs by means of small modifications of existing structures, with natural selection gradually weeding out those that prove themselves resistant to adaptation to new situations.

Consider for example the task of designing a device that collects visual information about the environment. Sight has been realized in numerous ways in living beings – by means of light-sensitive skin patches, pinhole eyes, facet eyes, tube eyes, camera eyes, and so on – and each kind of solution can have numerous shapes and structures (Schwab, 2018). Human eyes could for example have been considerably larger or smaller than they actually are, and it is at least physically possible to have a larger number of them. But individual solutions have varying advantages and disadvantages. Larger eyes, for instance, are able to capture more light than small eyes, thus providing better sight at low levels of illumination, but they are also more fragile and more costly (in terms of the organism's energy expenditure) to produce and maintain. And depending on its living circumstances, an organism may not actually need more than a particular level of eyesight. The solutions produced by natural selection accordingly incorporate trade-offs between different parameters without producing a single best solution for all kinds of organisms under all possible circumstances. Eyes evolved up to forty times independently, yielding a rich variety of workable solutions to the problem of sight and often with later solutions as modifications of earlier solutions (Schwab, 2018). These are not optimal in all aspects (think of the blind spot in human eyes due to the optic nerve passing through the retina, requiring the brain to supplement missing information), but nevertheless perform their task sufficiently well and have proven themselves sufficiently adaptable to new circumstances. Engineers looking for this type of solution can follow the example of natural selection by implementing its search algorithm.

The general algorithm is based on an abstract formulation of natural selection as an iteration of the creation of variation (through mutation, recombination, and sometimes drift) and selection proper (Dennett, 1995; Mitchell & Taylor, 1999: 593–594; Schurz, 2011: 131ff.; Miikulainen & Forrest, 2021: 9). The general algorithm originates in Lewontin's "Darwin's scheme" (Pennock, 2016: 782), discussed earlier.

Dennett (1995: 48ff.) was the first to point out that "Darwin's scheme" has an algorithmic structure and Godfrey-Smith (2009:19) conceives of it as a *recipe* for change.

But "Darwin's scheme" is too unspecific to serve as an algorithm or recipe that could be directly implemented. Dennett (1995: 51) suggests that "Darwin's scheme" can be thought of as a *general algorithm* (something like a rough sketch of an algorithmic structure) that defines a class of concrete algorithms that are built on the same coarse-grained structure but considerably differ in details and fit different cases. These specific algorithms can then be implemented *in silico* by defining a starting population of potential solutions to a set task, attributing fitness values to these that represent how well they perform, letting population members multiply according to these values (with fitter members producing more offspring) and eliminating those whose fitness values fall below a specified threshold, then allowing random mutations (and often recombination of solutions) to occur in the generation that was thus obtained, and using this as the starting population for the next iteration of the algorithm.[22]

Often a distinction is made between "phenotypes" and "genotypes" in a way that resembles the distinction in biology. Eiben & Smith (2015: 476) describe it as follows:

> At the higher level (the original problem context), phenotypes (candidate solutions) have their fitness measured. Selection mechanisms then use this measure to choose a pool of parents for each generation, and decide which parents and offspring go forward to the next generation. At the lower level, genotypes are objects that represent phenotypes in a form that can be manipulated to produce variations […]. Genotype-phenotype mapping bridges the two levels. At the genotypic level, variation operators generate new individuals (offspring) from selected parents.

In evolutionary computing (Schoenauer, 2015), the individuals in an evolving population are pieces of software code such that the algorithm is applied at the "genotype" (code) level. In evolutionary robotics (Bredeche, 2015), the individuals are physical robots with a phenotype (a set of traits) that are constructed on the basis of sets of instructions (their "genotype") evolving *in silico*.

The fields in focus here employ a strongly flattened description of biological evolution, namely a minimalist description of the conditions for

---

[22] The general algorithm is instantiated in several different techniques, such as evolutionary programming and genetic algorithms (Mitchell & Taylor, 1999; Schoenauer, 2015). Eiben & Smith (2015) and Schoenauer (2015) provide detailed descriptions of the algorithm.

natural selection processes to occur (i.e., "Darwin's scheme"). This description is somewhat richer than the view of evolution that underpins the Natural History Mode of crossover, in which only the *occurrence* of selection and descent feature as background assumptions but the dynamics of evolutionary processes and the conditions for selection to occur do not come into play. Note, too, that in the Algorithmic Mode such flattening is a *necessary* part of the strategy, as the approach rests on singling out natural selection as an effective and comparatively easily implementable method for searching solutions in large design spaces.

As in design contexts the aim often is to find optimal or near-optimal solutions for design problems (Mitchell & Taylor, 1999; Bredeche, 2015; Schoenauer, 2015; Winfield, 2024), the implementations of the general algorithm involve strongly idealized conditions. Natural selection *in principle* is an optimizing process: given a population of organisms in a specific environment, natural selection will cause the population to optimally adapt to the environment *if* the environment remains constant, the population is infinitely large, and the evolutionary process can take place over an infinite timespan. The first condition should be clear: if the environment changes while the population is evolving, it follows a moving target that it much harder to reach than a stationary one. The second condition may be somewhat harder to see: the reason is that in finite populations stochastic effects will occur that may push the evolving population off its course toward an optimal state. The third condition is to do with the fact that biological evolution depends on the mutations that arise from generation to generation, which means that there must be sufficient time for the necessary mutations to occur to open up a trajectory toward a state of optimal adaptedness. In real life, however, environments are always changing, populations are finite and time is limited, such that real-world populations usually do not reach states of optimal adaptation to environmental conditions, but rather states of *sufficient* adaptation. Implementations *in silico* are often designed as optimization processes, while natural selection in real biological populations is a satisficing rather than optimizing process (cf. Jacob, 1977).

As it hinges on a general algorithm that is abstracted away from the biological details and made concrete for specific cases, it seems that the Algorithmic Mode of crossover involves a procedure of "generalization and respecification" (Mayntz, 1997a; Section 2.1). But, as was already pointed out, "Darwin's scheme" is not a descriptive model of the process of natural selection but rather a specification of the conditions under which the process can occur. Mayntz's procedure thus does not apply here, I contend, as what is transferred falls short of being a model of natural selection. Moreover, natural selection is not equal to evolution and the epistemic content that is transferred into these fields thus cannot be conceived of as a description of biological evolution. Authors working in these fields themselves occasionally point out that the algorithm is "extremely simplified" (Schoenauer, 2015: 621) and falls short of describing biological evolution in a number of respects (Miikulainen & Forrest, 2021). While this does not constitute a practical problem for these fields with respect to achieving their aims, it does mean that they only align with specific ways of understanding evolution.

By focusing on natural selection, the Algorithmic Mode fits the ultra-selectionism of Wallace's and Weismann's Neo-Darwinism, as well as the Gene's-Eye View of Evolution, but misaligns with the other views discussed in Section 3. While for instance phenotypic plasticity and niche construction are increasingly taken into account in implementations of the general algorithm (Ziemke et al., 2004; Clune et al., 2007; Fortuna, 2022), this is done in a less integrative way than in approaches to an Extended Synthesis. While a central thesis of an Extended Synthesis is that organisms can cause biases to selection processes by means of phenotypic plasticity and niche construction, and in this way introduce a degree of directionality in evolution, in the Algorithmic Mode of crossover phenotypic plasticity and niche construction are mostly investigated as products of artificial evolution that contribute to the functionality of designs (i.e., their inbuilt ability to continue to perform their function under changeable conditions) and less as causal factors in evolutionary processes themselves. In this respect, the current debates on a possible Extended Synthesis can provide important impulses for developing new avenues for research in the Algorithmic Mode of crossover.

Note that research in the Algorithmic Mode also crosses back into biology. Evolutionary algorithms can be used as models to study natural selection in the (digital) laboratory (Wilke & Adami, 2002; Fortuna, 2022; Winfield, 2024), for instance by generating hypotheses regarding what in specific circumstances would have been an optimal trait (Mitchell & Taylor, 1999; Pennock, 2016). Such hypotheses can then be tested against actual traits found in natural populations, with divergences between the optimal trait and actually realized traits providing insight into the evolutionary processes that may have occurred in the lineages of which these populations are part. An evolutionary algorithm has also been used to answer a persistent challenge to evolutionary theory, namely that the theory would be unable to explain how the machine-like, functional complex organization of organisms (one of Darwin's main explananda in the

Origin – see Section 3.1) could have originated through natural selection of less complex features. This challenge – the challenge of "irreducible complexity" (Behe, 2004) – is often levied against evolutionary theory by proponents of so-called "Intelligent Design." By letting digital "organisms" (self-replicating computer programs that mutate and compete for energy units needed to carry out instructions) evolve under controlled circumstances, researchers showed that evolution can in principle explain this phenomenon (Lenski et al., 2003).

While the Algorithmic Mode rests on the use of a general algorithm that is inspired by the central search process in biological evolution, it does not consist in the application of a model of biological evolution. What is applied is highly idealized, general – and because of its generality, heuristically useful – description of natural selection. A fortiori, and *pace* Dennett (1995), the Algorithmic Mode of crossover cannot be understood as an application of evolutionary *theory* in non-biological fields, as evolutionary theorizing is much richer and more pluralistic than the abstract algorithm of natural selection. Yet, important connections between evolutionary biology and fields that involve an algorithmic view of selection can be made, and crossovers go in both directions.

4.3 Evolution as Generalized Science: Transferring Explanatory Content

What I call the *Generalized Science Mode* of crossover is found in various areas of the social sciences, conceived of broadly, such as evolutionary economics, evolutionary organization science, and evolutionary studies of science and technology. The central assumption underlying this mode of crossover is that biological evolution consists of a set of very specific instantiations of a more general process that can be instantiated throughout a wide range of domains.[23] Accordingly, it would be possible to generalize the explanatory framework of biological evolutionary theory into a broad theory that covers instances of evolution in any domain in which these occur.

Generalizing this framework is understood as a bottom-up process in which researchers seek out similarities between phenomena in different domains that would allow these to be covered by the same theory, "a *general* over-arching explanatory framework for beginning to understand the evolution of all these systems" (Aldrich et al., 2008: 578; original

---

[23] Schulz (2020: 10ff.) calls this the "structural form" of evolutionary economics.

emphasis). However, the process is not unbiased. Not all potential cases of evolution from various domains are treated on a par, but the search for relevant similarities is guided by the well-known paradigmatic cases of evolution found in biology. Researchers need paradigmatic cases to know what to look for in other domains, after all. Accordingly, the explanatory framework of biological evolutionary theorizing is taken as the framework from which generalization efforts start.

To illustrate this mode of crossover, I will discuss a research program that features prominently in evolutionary economics, namely Generalized Darwinism (Aldrich et al., 2008; Hodgson, 2003; 2009; 2019; Hodgson & Knudsen, 2006; 2008; 2010). I am aware that this is merely one approach in a much more diverse field, but I believe Generalized Darwinism nicely illustrates the Generalized Science Mode (and for reasons of space I have to limit the discussion to this one case). Critical discussions of Generalized Darwinism have been provided by Reydon (2021), Reydon & Scholz (2009; 2014; 2015), Scholz & Reydon (2013), and Schulz (2020).

Generalized Darwinism aims to explain the diversity and structures of complex economic and social entities (Hodgson, 2019: 24–25), that is, organizational forms, in the same way as biological evolutionary theory explains organismal forms. Generalized Darwinism is highly visible as an approach within evolutionary economics, but its proponents conceive of it more broadly as an approach to social and cultural evolution generally. The program's proponents point out that their approach does not involve using human evolutionary history to obtain knowledge about human nature that could inform social and economic issues (Hodgson & Knudsen, 2008: 52), as is done in the Natural History Mode of crossover. They also insist that their program does not involve a transfer of theoretical content from biology into economics, but rather is independent of biological theorizing. This latter claim, however, seems difficult to uphold: biological evolutionary theorizing clearly serves as a role model for theory building in Generalized Darwinism in a way that *prima facie* looks like an instance of Mayntz's (1992; 1997a; 1997b) procedure of generalization and respecification. Let me explain.

Generalized Darwinism starts from the assumption of an "ontological communality" (Aldrich et al., 2008: 579; Hodgson, 2009: xiv; Hodgson & Knudsen, 2010: 22) or "common ontological ground" (Hodgson & Knudsen, 2008: 51) between biological evolution and evolution in the economic and social domain. The assumption here is not that biological and socioeconomic evolution have the same fine-grained ontology, but rather that their coarse-grained structures are the same, such that they can be considered instantiations of the same general category of processes of which instantiations in various domains differ in the details wen described at more fine-grained levels (Reydon & Scholz, 2015: 566–567). Hodgson & Knudsen, for instance, explain that the fundamental assumption of Generalized Darwinism amounts to recognizing "common abstract features in both the social and the biological world" (2010: 22), which involve "ontological differences at the level of detail, [but] nevertheless, also common ontological features at an abstract level" (2010: 38). Hodgson explains that

> underneath the very real differences of character and mechanism, biological evolution and economic evolution might have types of process or structure in common, when considered at a sufficiently general level of abstraction. [...] These identical types of process or structure [...] point to common concepts or mechanisms, such as those at the core of Darwinism (2003: 366–367).

The authors argue that this enables them to develop domain-specific evolutionary theories on the basis of a general Darwinian framework that specifies general principles of evolution (Hodgson & Knudsen, 2008; Hodgson, 2009; 2019: 29). Such domain-specific evolutionary theories are taken as having explanatory force: the aim is to explain economic and social phenomena using the same explanatory structure as biological evolutionary theory provides for the explanation of biological phenomena (*ibid.*).

Generalized Darwinism invokes a minimalist conceptual formulation of evolution by natural selection that is also central in the Algorithmic Mode of crossover, namely "Darwin's scheme." It assumes a basic ontology of populations of entities that vary and are replicated (Hodgson, 2009: xii; 2019: 27, 31; Hodgson & Knudsen, 2006: 16; 2010; 4–9, 18–19, 31–37) combined with the "core Darwinian principles of variation, selection and inheritance" (Hodgson & Knudsen, 2008: 51), or alternatively variation, selection and retention (Aldrich et al., 2008: 584; Hodgson & Knudsen, 2006: 5; 2010: 23, 34). The application of the conceptual framework is justified by the existence of ontological similarities between domains:[24]

> As long as there is a population of replicating entities with varying capacities to survive, then Darwinian evolution will occur. Social evolution deals with populations of entities, including customs and social institutions that compete for scarce resources. [...] Social evolution is Darwinian by virtue of (social) ontology, not (biological) analogy (Hodgson & Knudsen, 2006: 16; also Hodgson, 2019: 31; Hodgson & Knudsen, 2008: 57; 2010: 46; Aldrich et al., 2008: 585).

---

[24] Note how this argument resonates with Kuhlmann's (2019) point that structural similarities underpin the successful application of models from physics in economics (Section 2.1).

The authors thus explicitly conceive of their own approach as not relying on analogies between the living and the social/economic worlds, as they take a justification of the conceptual framework to require more than drawing analogies (cf. Section 1.2).[25]

Here important differences surface between the Generalized Science Mode and the Algorithmic Mode of crossover. Approaches in the Algorithmic Mode aim to find solutions in large search spaces, while approaches in the Generalized Science Mode aim to explain outcomes of evolutionary processes. Accordingly, while both use Lewontin's "Darwin's scheme" as the basis for constructing domain-specific applications, it performs different roles in these two modes of crossover. In the Algorithmic Mode, "Darwin's scheme" serves as a heuristic for constructing algorithms *in silico* and a set of criteria that can be used to evaluate these algorithms. In the Generalized Science Mode, it is used as an explanatory model of evolution. But because describing and explaining phenomena that are found in the world is a very different kind of endeavor than constructing algorithms to search large solution spaces, the Generalized Science Mode must make ontological commitments that the Algorithmic Mode does not have to make and hence faces challenges that the Algorithmic Mode does not face.

The possibility of formulating causal explanations in the social and economic domain that are structurally similar to causal explanations in evolutionary biology presupposes the transfer of explanatory models of evolution between fields, as discussed in Section 2.1. Recall that for the generalization and respecification involved in model transfer to be successful, the ontologies of the source and target domains should not be too different. But it is far from clear that the ontologies of the biological and the socioeconomic domains are sufficiently similar to allow the transfer of explanatory models. Researchers in fields that instantiate the Generalized Science Mode thus are constrained by the actual ontologies of the source and target fields, whereas researchers in fields instantiating the Algorithmic Mode can freely design search algorithms that meet Lewontin's requirements without much regard for such ontological issues. For the former researchers, the crucial question is whether the ontology of their field sufficiently maps onto the ontology of evolutionary biology, whereas for the latter researchers, the question is whether they can devise algorithms that meet Lewontin's criteria. The latter, I suspect, is an easier issue to address than the former.

---

[25] They also emphasize that their approach does not involve the reduction of social and economic phenomena to biological ones (Hodgson & Knudsen, 2010: 21).

Indeed, Hodgson admits that for the case of Generalized Darwinism "[t]he question is whether the appropriate social and natural ontologies share sufficient features in common at some fundamental level" (2003: 366). There are reasons to doubt that the answer is affirmative (Reydon & Scholz, 2015; Scholz & Reydon, 2013). Proponents of Generalized Darwinism insist that their approach applies to "population[s] of replicating entities with varying capacities to survive" (Hodgson & Knudsen, 2006: 16) or "complex population systems" (Hodgson, 2019: 29; Hodgson & Knudsen, 2010). But the populations that are in focus are not the sort of entities that can undergo evolution in the way biological populations do (Reydon & Scholz, 2015; Scholz & Reydon, 2013).

In Generalized Darwinism, populations of social or economic entities are defined on the basis of typology and extension as groups of organizations of the same type that operate at a particular location. Types of social and economic entities are "similar in key respects" (Hodgson & Knudsen, 2006: 4; 2010: 32–33; Aldrich et al., 2008: 582) and are defined by their specific ways of operating in their social and business environments. Examples of such types are types of financial institutions, firms, small businesses, restaurants, local government offices, volunteer organizations, and so on. Invoking a biological parallel, such types could be understood as the socioeconomic equivalents of species roles in ecosystems (e.g., decomposers, predators, and pollinators). Investment banks and consumer banks, for instance, are types of financial institutions that each operate in their own way, which is typical for the kind of banks they are. The populations in Generalized Darwinism then are groups such as all consumer banks that operate in a particular region.

But while this makes for a possibly insightful ecological analogy, it jars with a view of populations as evolving entities. While there is some debate about the precise nature of biological populations (Reydon & Scholz, 2015, and references therein), it is clear that biological populations are *systems* of organisms that are connected by reproductive, cooperative and competitive interactions, and separated from other populations by restricted flow of genetic material between them. Restricted gene flow is important for the possibility of novel traits to spread through the population without being "watered down" by constant influx of genetic material from the outside. Biological evolving populations are reproductive communities or gene pools that are sufficiently separated from each other (Reydon & Scholz, 2015: 576).

To see this, consider Godfrey-Smith's (2009) notion of "Darwinian populations," which is based on Lewontin's three principles that are also central in Generalized Darwinism. For Godfrey-Smith, Darwinian populations are those entities that have the capacity to undergo evolution by means of natural selection, where a "Darwinian population is a collection of entities in which there is variation in character, the inheritance of some of those characteristics, and differences in how much individuals reproduce" (Godfrey-Smith, 2009: 110). Godfrey-Smith highlights reproduction as a core aspect of Darwinian evolution (2009: 69ff.) and gives reproduction a central place as a criterion for a population to have the capacity to evolve: the members of a Darwinian population must be bound together in the population by means of reproductive relations for the population to be capable of evolving. Even though organisms constitute populations in different ways – microbes, oaks, slime molds, and gorillas are different kinds of beings that interact in different ways and have different ways of passing on traits to the next generation – there is broad agreement among biologists that all evolving populations are systems of organisms that must exhibit sufficient degrees of interconnectedness between members, internal cohesion, and closure[26] for them to be able to participate as wholes in evolutionary processes (for detailed discussion, see Reydon & Scholz, 2015: 575–581; Scholz & Reydon, 2013: 996–997). That is, that ontologically biological populations are *individuals* (Millstein, 2009; 2010; Reydon & Scholz, 2015: 580).

Sets of organisms (in biology) or of organizations (in Generalized Darwinism) that are defined typologically are not individuals in this sense and accordingly cannot function as units of evolution in evolutionary processes (for a detailed argument, see Reydon & Scholz, 2015). In this respect, the ontology of Generalized Darwinism mismatches with the ontology of biological evolution, calling into doubt the assumption of ontological communality on which the program rests. To some extent, the issue may be due to the fact that the term "population" in biology has multiple meanings and biologists themselves often fail to specify its meaning (Reydon & Scholz, 2015; Scholz & Reydon, 2013). For instance, while proponents of Generalized Darwinism assert to follow Mayr's "population thinking," Hey (2011) shows that the population concept in Mayr's perspective does not in fact refer to units that undergo evolution. Abrams (2023: 117ff.) argues that biologists often use less strict conceptions of populations than the view that populations are individuals in the sense discussed earlier.

---

[26] In the sense of a high level of gene exchange within the population and a sufficiently low level with other populations for the population to have its own evolutionary fate (Millstein, 2009: 269; 2010: 66; Reydon & Scholz, 2015: 578).

Be that as it may, the challenge for proponents of Generalized Darwinism is to identify populations in the social and economic domains that are ontologically sufficiently similar to biological populations, whatever biologists think populations are. This a challenge that I believe so far has not been met, but that should not be impossible to meet.

Note that this challenge manifests itself in different ways depending on the formulation of "Darwin's scheme" that is used. Various putative summaries of evolution in triplet form besides Lewontin's "Darwin's scheme" are in circulation (see Godfrey-Smith, 2009: 17ff.) For example, while Lewontin's formulation encompasses variation, survival and reproduction, and inheritance (Lewontin, 1970; Godfrey-Smith, 2007; 2009: 17–20; Ågren, 2021, 68–72; Section 2.2), theoretical biologist Martin Nowak (2006a: 9) specifies the triplet replication–selection–mutation as the defining principles of evolutionary dynamics. Researchers in evolutionary sociology, evolutionary economics, and related fields often use a still different triplet that highlights *retention* instead of reproduction: variation–selection–retention (e.g., Campbell, 1960; 1965; Nelson, 2007; Stoelhorst, 2008a; 2008b; Smaldino & McElreath, 2016; Smaldino, 2022).[27] And Lewontin (2010) in a later publication added a fourth principle to his "Darwin's scheme," the principle of mutation, noting that this was required to explain the origin of novel forms.[28] While formulations like these are often understood as brief, concise summaries of evolution by natural selection, they present quite different pictures and it is important to ask what exactly they are pictures of.

According to Hodgson and Knudsen, "Darwinian evolution involves the development, retention, and selection of information concerning adaptive solutions to survival problems faced by entities in their environment" (Hodgson & Knudsen, 2010: 42, 46, 230), and they connect this to the replicator–interactor framework of the Gene's-Eye View (e.g., Hodgson & Knudsen 2010: ix, 24, 61, 65, 85–88). For instance, the evolution of firms and other organizations is conceptualized in terms of routines, rules, and other units of behavior (as it were, the "genes" underlying organizational behaviors) that are transmitted between organizations (the organizational equivalents of organisms) and can be retained in the population or not. But while invoking retention of entities instead of reproduction does make it easier to conceive of populations as sets (of genes, routines, or other

---

[27] Campbell (1960; 1965) refers to variation and selective retention, thus suggesting that selection is a specific mode of retention. Note, too, that Lewontin's triplet is a specification of conditions *for* natural selection, while other triplets *include* selection.

[28] Cf. Section 2.2 on the question what selection can explain.

units of information), reproduction in a breeding or a clonal population is not the same as the mere retention of entities in a set. Even on a permissive conceptualization of reproduction (such as for instance Godfrey-Smith, 2009, advocates) organisms reproducing at different rates due to environmental pressures instantiate a different mechanism from the one Hodgson and Knudsen, and other proponents of the variation–selection–retention triplet consider (information being retained on the basis of usefulness in a particular environment).

In the same way as the Algorithmic Mode of crossover, the focus on natural selection locates the Generalized Science Mode closer to Neo-Darwinist ultra-selectionism and the Gene's-Eye View of evolution than to the other, more pluralistic views discussed in Section 3. But the use of triplets that include retention rather than reproduction puts approaches in the Generalized Science Mode at some distance from biological evolution. Not only does Lewontin's "Darwin's scheme" fall considerably short of constituting an explanatory model of evolution, or even of natural selection, that can be applied to describe and explain economic and social phenomena – it is debatable whether a scheme that includes retention rather than reproduction even connects well to natural selection. This is a debate that is actually taking place: recently some biologists and philosophers have begun to argue that reproduction is not a necessary requirement for evolution by means of natural selection and proposed modifications of Lewontin's scheme to accommodate a view of natural selection without reproduction (for an introduction to the literature and an argument in favor of this view, see Papale, 2021). The outcome of this debate remains to be seen, but it will certainly have consequences for the options available to proponents of the Generalized Science Mode of crossover.

The focus on retention rather than reproduction will also affect the possibilities for bringing approaches in the Generalized Science Mode closer to thoroughly pluralistic views of evolution. Integrating causal factors such as phenotypic plasticity and niche construction into evolutionary explanations requires a view of evolution in which organisms play a central role as the entities that can bias the direction of evolutionary processes by changing their phenotypes or changing their selective environments (Section 3). In Generalized Darwinism, the parallel entities would presumably be institutions and there indeed are good reasons to emphasize the phenotypic plasticity and niche construction of institutions as causal factors in an evolutionary approach to explaining the properties and behaviors of economic and social entities. Firms, for instance, actively try to construct their niches by way of marketing efforts and actively change their ways of operating in response to the environments in which they operate. But while such activities of course are recognized, they are not integrated in a pluralistic picture of evolutionary processes in ways discussed under the header of an Extended Synthesis. Moreover, shorthand formulations of evolution in terms of the retention of units of information eclipse the active role of social and economic entities rather than foregrounding them, in the same way as the Gene's-Eye View strongly eclipses organisms from the description of how evolution works. While proponents of Generalized Darwinism and other approaches in the Generalized Science Mode may of course choose to model their approach on the Gene's-Eye View rather than more pluralistic views, it should at least be clear that by doing this their approach may stand at considerable distance from the way biologists explain evolutionary phenomena and thus may not necessarily warrant the epithet "evolutionary."

Generalized Darwinism at present is the best developed approach in the Generalized Science Mode of crossover, and for that reason I have used it to illustrate the general aspects of this kind of crossover.[29] It is also one of the few approaches that in a full-fledged manner instantiates the Generalized Science Mode by considering evolutionary theory to be a general theory of population change and the origin of complex organization that covers phenomena in many different domains. In the literature, terms such as "generalized evolutionary theory" are used in a broad sense to discuss a large diversity of approaches, many of which do not instantiate this – or for that matter, any – mode of crossover (for overviews, see Baraghith & Feldbacher-Escamilla, 2021; Baraghith, 2022). But the example of Generalized Darwinism also serves well to show which challenges the Generalized Science Mode of crossover faces. In this respect, I hope the preceding discussion has clarified some of what could be done to further develop this mode of crossover and help it achieve its full potential.

5 The Evolutionary Style of Thinking

5.1 Biological Styles of Thinking

The preceding sections showed that crossovers from evolutionary biology into other fields should not be understood in terms of evolutionary *theory* being applied to a new category of phenomena. One mode rests on the use of knowledge from the evolutionary history of the human species, while the other two modes involve the use of a very general formulation of the criteria under which natural selection can occur, that is too

---

[29] For broader coverage in economics, see Schulz (2020: 37–66).

minimalistic in several aspects to be conceived of as an explanatory model of the evolutionary process as such, or even a model of the process of natural selection. All involve strongly flattened views of evolution. So, how do these modes of crossover result in fields of research that can properly be considered *evolutionary*? Is there a unifying factor?

I want to sketch the outlines of a perspective that I believe can illuminate what is evolutionary about the various fields and approaches that self-identify as such, and that enables us to better understand how crossovers from biology into other areas of science and scholarship work than the account discussed in Section 2.1. I contend that crossovers are best understood as involving the application of a particular style of thinking and not of a particular scientific theory – what is transferred is evolutionary *thinking*, not evolutionary *theory*. The term "evolutionary thinking" is not new (cf. Buskes, 2006; Heams et al., 2015; Du Crest et al., 2023) and is often used loosely to refer to a "family of ways of thinking about living things […] that began with the work of Charles Darwin" (Depew & Weber, 1995: 1). I have a more technical usage in mind, however, that brings out the contrast between theory transfer and transferring a style of thinking.

I start from recent work by Currie (2021), who notes that life can be studied from a number of different perspectives, without there being a unique, best perspective that would capture all aspects of life. According to Currie, perspectives for studying life are embodied in different styles of thinking about life, where a "style of thinking involves a paradigm kind of explanation, a set of related tools, and an associated, more ephemeral 'perspective'" (Currie, 2021: 28), or a "canonical explanatory schema and an accompanying perspective or point of view" (Currie, 2021: 6). A perspective on a particular kind of phenomena under investigation thus follows from the particular kind of explanation that is sought for them. Different kinds of explanation entail different perspectives on the subject matter under study, each making it appear as a different kind of phenomena. Currie points to a number of such styles of thinking in the biological sciences, including comparative thinking, population thinking, and homology thinking. He does not develop the notion in detail and there are marked differences between the styles he discusses (Currie, 2021: 27–29). Still, Currie's work constitutes a good starting point to develop my suggestion that evolutionary thinking is best understood as a general style of thinking about a specific kind of subject matter.[30]

---

[30] Elsewhere (Desmond et al., 2024) we use "style of reasoning" but do not develop this in detail.

To clarify Currie's notion, a contrast will be helpful with similar notions that feature prominently in the philosophy of science: Fleck's ([1935] 1979) "thought styles" ("*Denkstile*"), Crombie's (1994; 1996) "styles of thinking" and Hacking's (2002: 159–199) "styles of reasoning." For these authors, styles involve generally applicable, abstract methodologies for investigating the world and reasoning about the world.[31] Crombie, for example, highlights "hypothetical modelling" and "probabilistic and statistical analysis" as styles of thinking, and Hacking discusses "laboratory style." These are general ways of conducting research, revolving around a particular, often abstract *investigative methodology* that can be used to investigate a variety of phenomena throughout the sciences. Crombie's "hypothetical modelling," for example, refers to the method of clarifying structural or behavioral properties of some unknown system by simulating it using material artifacts (e.g., scale models or specifically prepared model organisms) or theoretical artifacts (sets of differential equations, computer simulations, etc.) of which the properties are already well known (Crombie, 1996: 74). Similarly, Hacking's (2002: 184) "laboratory style" is a general way of doing experiments that involves two layers of modeling: constructing a model of the phenomenon under investigation (the experimental setup in the laboratory) while using models of the laboratory equipment to understand how the setup models the phenomenon under investigation.

The styles of thinking Currie discusses contrast with Fleck's, Crombie's, and Hacking's styles by not revolving around a widely applicable investigative method, but around the specific subject matter and epistemic content of biology. Biological styles of thinking trace one or several specifically biological kinds of phenomena that are explained in a specific way. Homology thinking, for instance, traces a particular kind of explicitly biological phenomena: shared traits explained by common ancestry. Similarly, population thinking traces changes in trait and gene frequencies in populations explained by selection, drift, mutation, and migration (cf. Hey, 2011). And comparative thinking on Currie's view traces a pluralistic kind of biological phenomena, namely trait similarities that can be due to any combination of common ancestry, convergent or parallel evolution, developmental constraints, and trait evolvability, tracing these in an integrative manner. Comparative thinking thus does not trace similarities and differences between organisms of different

---

[31] Sciortino (2017) provides a clear discussion of the similarities and differences between Fleck's, Crombie's, and Hacking's notions.

groups *per se*, but similarities and differences that are due to the same underlying causal complex and therefore can be explained within the same (in this case pluralistic) explanatory framework. Fleck's, Crombie's, and Hacking's styles trace affordances provided by general methodologies, whereas Currie's styles of thinking trace parts of the content of biological science, namely a category of phenomena combined with a kind of explanation that is sought for them.

A style of thinking in Currie's sense thus has an epistemological element – the identification of a category of phenomena that is guided by the specific kind of explanation that is being sought for them – and an ontological element – an account of the nature of the phenomena that are being traced and of the factors that cause them. Conceiving of evolutionary thinking as a style of thinking in this sense yields a perspective that avoids pressing issues that arise when understanding crossovers as involving the travel of a theory between fields, such as the precise content of the theory that is allegedly traveling and the availability of explanatory models of the evolutionary process, and better accommodates the disunity and explanatory pluralism that has been inherent in evolutionary theorizing from the beginning. The central questions now are what kind(s) of biological phenomena and what kind(s) of explanatory factors evolutionary thinking traces.

5.2 Thinking about Form

Section 3 provides a first answer to these questions. The phenomena listed in Table 1 constitute a diverse lot and so do the explanatory factors listed in Table 2. But there is unity in diversity here that allows us to conceive of evolutionary thinking as tracing a specific category of biological phenomena that are explained using a specific kind of scientific explanation. Let me clarify.

The phenomena listed in Table 1 all are aspects of *organismal form*, or at least phenomena directly related to organismal form (such as the geographical distribution of forms).[32] Here, "form" is understood in a broad sense. The kind of phenomena in focus in evolutionary theorizing consist of various aspects of the physiological structures, and of the morphological and behavioral traits of living beings: their origins, their functional organization, their internal and external adaptedness, the similarities within groups and differences between groups, and their geographical distribution and succession in time. In the *Origin*, Darwin often refers to

---

[32] For this point, see for example Müller & Newman (2003).

the various "forms of life" as the phenomena in focus in his work and he famously ends the *Origin* by stating how his view of life shows how "endless forms most beautiful and most wonderful" (Darwin, 1859: 490) have come into being. Changes in allele and trait frequencies – the population-level phenomena that came into focus in the Modern Synthesis, the Gene's-Eye View and the Neutral Theory – are less of interest for their own sake, but are important as what underlies changes in organismal traits and structures, and the origin of evolutionary novelties. In the end, this is what biological evolutionary theorizing has always been about: explaining the various aspects of organismal forms.[33]

In accounting for organismal forms, evolutionary thinking is guided by a particular kind of ideal explanatory structure that was introduced by Darwin and has been at the core of evolutionary theorizing ever since. Recall that Darwin invokes two "great laws" to explain organismal forms: natural selection and common descent (Section 3.1). By foregrounding these explanatory factors, Darwin highlights the two indispensable components of evolutionary explanations: process and history. Only invoking selection as an account of how evolutionary processes typically occur, as is often the case in crossovers, doesn't yield an adequate explanation of organismal forms – explanations must take the history of forms into account too. As discussed in Section 3.1, common descent provides crucial support for selection explanations, but for Darwin also counts as an explanatory factor in itself.

History is in a number of ways a crucial component of evolutionary explanations. This is because evolutionary biology does not explain traits and trait distributions in isolation, but explains evolutionary novelties and changes in trait distributions *in relation to* ancestral traits and distributions – the questions in focus are how the evolutionary trajectory from an ancestral trait to a descendant trait actually occurred and what circumstances made the trajectory possible in the first place (Reydon, 2023). Evolutionary trajectories are constrained by both the environmental circumstances and the population's composition at that time (Dupré, 2003: 33–34). The composition of the population (i.e., the composition of the gene or trait pool) is a crucial factor regarding the possible trajectories that can be taken while at the same time being a product of the

---

[33] Arguably, organismal forms have constituted the principal explanandum of biology since Aristotle. And notwithstanding a contemporary focus on the molecular level, the overarching aim of evolutionary biology still is to understand "these elaborately constructed forms" (Darwin, 1859: 489) and the explananda Darwin had in view were all connected to organismal form.

population's evolutionary history. As Dupré (2003: 20) puts it aptly: "where one can go depends more than anything else on where one is, and on how one got there." Note, though, that this is not merely a matter of the historical situation constraining the population's evolutionary trajectory, but also of opening up possible trajectories for the evolving population to take (Reydon, 2023). Evolution builds novelties on the basis of existing traits and structures, such that the availability of traits and structures also makes certain innovations possible. In these respects, organismal forms can only be understood in relation to the ancestral forms from which they were modified and without which the emergence of a new trait or structure would not have been possible. Evolution is a tinkerer (Jacob, 1977), who by trial and error finds new ways of doing things.

Accordingly, the kind of scientific explanation that evolutionary thinking traces, *evolutionary explanation*, can be characterized as consisting of a processual and a historical component, where the former specifies those factors that caused the evolutionary trajectory leading to the organismal forms under study to occur in a particular manner, and the latter specifies those factors that constrained the trajectory and made it possible in the first place.[34] While this is a fairly coarse-grained account of the structure of evolutionary explanations, it is not more coarse grained than other general accounts of specific kinds of scientific explanation, such as the Deductive-Nomological and mechanistic accounts (Woodward & Ross, 2021). In a similar way as those accounts, it explicates the general structure of a particular mode of scientific explanation and guides researchers regarding the kinds of components that are required to build adequate explanations in that mode. For instance, the Deductive-Nomological account tells researchers that when aiming to devise law-based explanations of the phenomena they study, they should specify the relevant laws of nature and the initial conditions from which a description of those phenomena can be deduced. The mechanistic account tells researchers that they should specify the relevant entities involved in the phenomena under consideration and their interactions, and show how these interactions produce the phenomena to be explained. Similarly, the characterization of evolutionary explanation as a generic kind of scientific explanation consisting of a processual and a historical component tells researchers what must be done to fully explain a specific category of phenomena – organismal form – in a specific way: they should specify the causal factors underlying

---

[34] Elsewhere (Reydon, 2023), I elaborate this account of evolutionary explanations in detail. Here I can only provide a very brief summary.

the evolutionary trajectory from a particular ancestral form to the form to be explained, as well as the historical factors that constrained the trajectory and opened it up.

This is not to say that complete evolutionary explanations are what evolutionary biology commonly produces, nor that these are even what evolutionary biologists aim for. Philosophers of biology have long noted that evolutionary biology encompasses a considerable diversity of modes of explanation and there is no single mode of explanation that all explanations in evolutionary biology strictly conform to (Reydon, 2023: 163; Gildenhuys, 2024). Evolutionary biology features selection explanations, developmental explanations, lineage explanations, homology explanations, topological explanations, and more. These different kinds of explanation can be seen as providing partial explanations of evolutionary phenomena, each tracing a different kind of causal factor. Depending on the case under consideration, different kinds of explanation may be relevant and taken together these may constitute a complete evolutionary explanation of that case. (Note how the fact that evolutionary biologists use a multitude of explanations fits the intrinsic pluralism of evolutionary thinking, highlighted in Section 3.) In concrete research projects, researchers typically focus on one aspect of a phenomenon, for instance what the contribution of natural selection was to a specific trait, or how developmental constraints played a role in its formation, and accordingly focus on one kind of explanation. Yet, even though evolutionary biologists do not typically aim for complete evolutionary explanations, I contend that in the background the general ideal of evolutionary explanation guides their thinking about the phenomena under consideration and constitutes the unifying background of research in the field.

I want to suggest that evolutionary thinking as laid out above can be extended to constitute a covering account for evolutionary fields and approaches in the broadest sense. In the same way as biological evolutionary theory is about specific aspects of organismal form (their functional organization, adaptedness, and so on), evolutionary thinking in this extended sense is about specific aspects of the *forms of entities* found in the world but cannot be explained completely (or not at all, in the case of most organisms) as products of human design. Evolutionary thinking traces the phenomenon of form in combination with the only kind of naturalistic explanation (apart from human design) that is available for this phenomenon, that is, evolutionary explanation.

The three modes of crossover that I distinguished can be interpreted as exemplifying evolutionary thinking in different ways. All three pertain to the forms of biological as well as non-biological entities. The Natural History Mode is concerned with the historical foundations of specific aspects of the organismal form of human beings: behavioral and mental traits that matter in society, politics, human history, and so on. The Algorithmic Mode is concerned with modeling the process of natural selection to find optimal – or at least satisficing – forms for various artificial entities that must perform specific tasks: pieces of software, robots, electronic circuits, and so on. The Generalized Science Mode is concerned with explaining the forms of various kinds of social and economic entities found in the world – firms, institutions, and so on – in the same way as organismal forms are explained, in a similar way as biological evolutionary theory explains organismal forms.

What makes the fields and approaches that self-identify as "evolutionary" into evolutionary fields and approaches, thus, is that they are concerned with identifying forms of entities that seem functionally organized, well adapted to their environments, and so on, and explaining these without invoking design as the explanation. They apply evolutionary thinking in various ways and in so doing take up a style of thinking that originated in biological science and is deeply entrenched there, and transpose it to non-biological fields of science and scholarship. Such crossovers do not fit the "model transfer" perspective discussed in Section 2.1, but constitute a different kind of scientific phenomenon that largely still awaits analysis by philosophers of science.

5.3 Where from Here?

I have only been able to discuss a few examples from the overwhelmingly rich spectrum of evolutionary approaches and fields. Yet I hope to have offered a perspective on the phenomenon of theory crossover that is more illuminating and more adequate to the complicated case of evolutionary thinking than the "model transfer" perspective from which philosophers of science often analyze the travel of theories, and that can open up new avenues of research in both the philosophy of science and evolutionary fields.

For philosophers of science, the perspective I offered shifts attention away from the question how scientific theories can be applied outside their home domain. That question immediately raises traditional philosophical questions regarding the nature of evolutionary theory as a scientific theory, its structure, core laws and principles, its constituent models, and so on – questions that are also central in the "model transfer" perspective but, I have suggested, are not the key issues when it comes to understanding the case of evolutionary thinking. Only one mode of crossover, the Generalized Science Mode, comes close to involving applications of an evolutionary theory throughout various fields, but faces considerable challenges. All modes of crossover involve strongly flattened views that reduce the evolutionary process to the barest bones of natural selection. Understanding the variety of evolutionary fields and approaches listed in Section 1 as resting on applications of a well-established scientific theory to a broad variety of phenomena thus is not a suitable approach and an alternative is needed. I have sketched the outlines of such an alternative that does justice to the rich tradition of evolutionary thinking from Darwin's work to present-day developments, and one task now is to develop it further by examining more cases.

Practitioners interested in implementing evolutionary approaches in their home field may benefit from this alternative perspective as it brings out the richness of evolutionary thinking and its ensuing versatility when it comes to explaining central aspects of the forms of entities in various domains of the natural, social, and artificial world. Evolutionary thinking as I conceive of it takes into account the whole tradition of evolutionary thinking from Darwin to the present rather than only considering presentations of evolutionary theory that align with the Gene's-Eye View or nineteenth-century ultra-selectionism. Such presentations represent stages in evolutionary theorizing that miss much of the explanatory pluralism that has been inherent in evolutionary theorizing ever since Darwin and that may well return to center stage if an Extended Synthesis establishes itself. Because all three basic modes of crossover from evolutionary theorizing into other areas of research involve strongly flattened representations of evolution, much of evolutionary thinking's potential remains untapped: instances of crossover that do not strongly focus on adaptation and selection but foreground other explananda and explanatory factors or that treat a plurality of explanatory factors in an integrative manner so far hardly exist. Here lies considerable potential for further development of evolutionary approaches outside biology by attempting to identify cases in which evolutionary explanatory factors other than selection play a prominent part in explaining phenomena under investigation.

But it is important to recall Dawkins' (2008) caution, mentioned in Section 1.2, when it comes to transferring evolutionary theory outside biology. In Section 4, I pointed to some – sometimes considerable – challenges for attempts at crossover, but I also attempted to highlight potential for further work. For the Natural History Mode the main challenges are to establish *that* certain human traits are innate and to assess what the innateness of a trait would mean for practice. The Generalized Science Mode faces the challenges to find adequate representations of the evolutionary process (instead of the triplet formulations that are commonly used) and to determine that a specific kind of non-biological process is ontologically sufficiently similar to biological evolutionary processes to count as a kind of evolutionary process.

Notwithstanding the existence of a diversity of fields and approaches that self-identify as "evolutionary," the scope of evolutionary thinking in the various areas of science and scholarship remains underexplored. Mapping out the prospects and pitfalls of evolutionary thinking in sufficient detail is a much-needed project – one for philosophers and evolutionary scientists and scholars to carry out in close collaboration.

References

Aaby, B. H., Dani, G., & Ramsey, G. (2024). Explanatory gaps in evolutionary theory. *Biology & Philosophy* 39: 22.

Abrams, M. (2023). *Evolution and the Machinery of Chance: Philosophy, Probability, and Scientific Practice in Biology*. Chicago: University of Chicago Press.

Ågren, J. A. (2021). *The Gene's-Eye View of Evolution*. Oxford: Oxford University Press.

Alberch, P. (1980). Ontogenesis and morphological diversification. *American Zoologist* 20: 653–667.

Aldrich, H. E., Hodgson, G. M., Hull, D. L., Knudsen, T., Mokyr, J., & Vanberg, V. J. (2008). In defence of generalized Darwinism. *Journal of Evolutionary Economics* 18: 577–596.

Allhoff, F. (2003). Evolutionary ethics from Darwin to Moore. *History and Philosophy of the Life Sciences* 25: 51–79.

André, J.-B., Cozic, M., De Monte, S., Gayon, J., Huneman, P., Martens, J., & Walliser, B. (2022). *From Evolutionary Biology to Economics and Back: Parallels and Crossings between Economics and Evolution*. Cham: Springer.

Baedke, J. (2025). *The Organism*. Cambridge: Cambridge University Press.

Baedke, J., Fábregas-Tejeda, A., & Vergara-Silva, F. (2020). Does the extended evolutionary synthesis entail extended explanatory power? *Biology & Philosophy* 35: 20.

Baraghith, K. (2022). *From Games to Graphs: Synthesizing Generalized Evolution Theory*. Paderborn: Brill Mentis.

Baraghith, K. & Feldbacher-Escamilla, C. J. (2021). The many faces of generalizing the theory of evolution. *American Philosophical Quarterly* 58: 35–49.

Barkow, J. H. (2006). Introduction: Sometimes the bus does wait. In J. H. Barkow (ed.), *Missing the Revolution: Darwinism for Social Scientists* (pp. 3–59). New York: Oxford University Press.

Basalla, G. (1988). *The Evolution of Technology*. Cambridge: Cambridge University Press.

Beatty, J. (1986). Pluralism and panselectionism. In P. D. Asquith & P. Kitcher (eds.), *PSA 1984: Proceedings of the Biennial Meetings of the Philosophy of Science Association*, Volume 2 (pp. 113–128). East Lansing: Philosophy of Science Association.

Beer, G. (2009). *Darwin's Plots: Evolutionary Narrative in Darwin, George Eliot and Nineteenth-Century Fiction* (Third Edition). Cambridge: Cambridge University Press.

Behe, M. (2004). Irreducible complexity: Obstacle to Darwinian evolution. In W. Dembski & M. Ruse (eds.), *Debating Design: From Darwin to DNA* (pp. 352–370). Cambridge: Cambridge University Press.

Birch, J. (2012). The negative view of natural selection. *Studies in History and Philosophy of Biological and Biomedical Sciences* 43: 596–573.

Borello, M. E. (2005). The rise, fall and resurrection of group selection. *Endeavour* 29: 43–47.

Boumans, M. (1993). Paul Ehrenfest and Jan Tinbergen: A case of limited physics transfer. *History of Political Economy* 25: 131–156.

Boumans, M. (2023). Materials selection in economic modeling. *Synthese* 201: 125.

Bowler, P. J. (1983). *The Eclipse of Darwinism: Anti-Darwinian Evolution Theories in the Decades Around 1900*. Baltimore: Johns Hopkins University Press.

Bowler, P. J. (2005). Variation from Darwin to the modern synthesis. In B. Hallgrímsson & B. K. Hall (eds.), *Variation* (pp. 9–27). Amsterdam: Elsevier.

Bowler, P. J. (2017). Alternatives to Darwinism in the early twentieth century. In R. G. Delisle (ed.), *The Darwinian Tradition in Context: Research Programs in Evolutionary Biology* (pp. 195–217). Cham: Springer.

Boyd, R. & Richerson, P. J. (1985). *Culture and the Evolutionary Process*. Chicago: University of Chicago Press.

Boyd, R. & Richerson, P. J. (2005). *The Origin and Evolution of Cultures*. New York: Oxford University Press.

Bradie, M. & Harms, W. (2023). Evolutionary epistemology. In E. N. Zalta & U. Nodelman (eds.), *Stanford Encyclopedia of Philosophy* (Spring 2023 Edition). https://plato.stanford.edu/archives/spr2023/entries/epistemology-evolutionary/.

Bredeche, N. (2015). Artificial evolution of autonomous robots and virtual creatures. In T. Heams, P. Huneman, G. Lecointre & M. Silberstein (eds.), *Handbook of Evolutionary Thinking in the Sciences* (pp. 637–646). Dordrecht: Springer.

Brey, P. (2008). Technological design as an evolutionary process. In P. E. Vermaas, P. Kroes, A. Light, & S. A. Moore (eds.), *Philosophy and Design: From Engineering to Architecture* (pp. 61–75). Dordrecht: Springer.

Brinkworth, M. & Weinert, F. (eds.) (2012). *Evolution 2.0: Implications of Darwinism in Philosophy and the Social and Natural Sciences*. Berlin: Springer.

Bull, J. J. & Wichman, H. A. (2001). Applied evolution. *Annual Review of Ecology and Systematics* 32: 183–217.

Buller, D. J. (2005). *Adapting Minds: Evolutionary Psychology and the Persistent Quest for Human Nature*. Cambridge, MA: MIT Press.

Burkhardt, R. W. (2013). Lamarck, evolution, and the inheritance of acquired characters. *Genetics* 194: 793–805.

Buskes, C. (2006). *Evolutionair Denken: De Invloed van Darwin op Ons Wereldbeeld*. Amsterdam: Nieuwezijds.

Butler, S. (1880). *Unconscious Memory*. London: David Bogue.

Calvin, M. (1965). Chemical evolution. *Proceedings of the Royal Society A* 288: 441–466.

Callebaut, W. (2011). Peering up above the Malthusian abyss. *Biological Theory* 6: 103–105.

Campbell, D. T. (1960). Blind variation and selective retentions in creative thought as in other knowledge processes. *Psychological Review* 67: 380–400.

Campbell, D. T. (1965). Variation and selective retention in socio-cultural evolution. In H. R. Barringer, G. I. Blankstein, & R. W. Mack (eds.), *Social Change in Developing Areas* (pp. 19–49). Cambridge, MA: Schenkman Publishing Company.

Carroll, J., McAdams, D. P., & Wilson, E. O. (eds.) (2016). *Darwin's Bridge: Uniting the Humanities & Sciences*. New York: Oxford University Press.

Cavalli-Sforza, L. L. & Feldman, M. W. (1981). *Cultural Transmission and Evolution: A Quantitative Approach*. Princeton: Princeton University Press.

Charbonneau, M. (ed.) (2024). *The Evolution of Techniques: Rigidity and Flexibility in Use, Transmission, and Innovation*. Cambridge, MA: MIT Press.

Charlat, S., Heams, T., & Rivoire, O. (2023). Is natural selection physical? In A. du Crest, M. Valkovic, A. Ariew, H. Desmond, P. Huneman, & T. A. C. Reydon (eds.), *Evolutionary Thinking across Disciplines: Problems and Perspectives in Generalized Darwinism* (pp. 287–296). Cham: Springer

Clavien, C. (2015). Evolution, society, and ethics: Social Darwinism versus evolutionary ethics. In T. Heams, P. Huneman, G. Lecointre, & M. Silberstein (eds.), *Handbook of Evolutionary Thinking in the Sciences* (pp. 725–745). Dordrecht: Springer.

Clune, J., Ofria, C., & Pennock, R. T. (2007). Investigating the emergence of phenotypic plasticity in evolving digital organisms. In F. Almeida e Costa, L. M. Rocha, E. Costa, I. Harvey, & A. Coutinho (eds.), *Advances in Artificial Life* (pp. 74–83). Berlin: Springer.

Crombie, A. C. (1994). *Styles of Thinking in the European Tradition (3 Volumes)*. London: Duckworth.

Crombie, A. C. (1996). Commitments and styles of European scientific thinking. *Theoria* 11: 65–76.

Currie, A. (2021). *Comparative Thinking in Biology*. Cambridge: Cambridge University Press.

Darwin, C. R. (1859). *On the Origin of Species by Means of Natural Selection, or the Preservation of Favoured Races in the Struggle for Life*. London: John Murray.

Darwin, C. R. (1909). *The Foundations of the Origin of Species: Two Essays Written in 1842 and 1844, Edited By His Son Francis Darwin*. Cambridge: Cambridge University Press.

Dawkins, R. (1982). Replicators and vehicles. In King's College Sociobiology Group (ed.), *Problems in Sociobiology* (pp. 45–64). Cambridge: Cambridge University Press.

Dawkins, R. (1983). Universal Darwinism. In D. S. Bendall (ed.), *Evolution from Molecules to Men* (pp. 403–425). Cambridge: Cambridge University Press.

Dawkins, R. (2008). Why Darwin matters. *The Guardian*, Friday 8 February 2008.

De Smedt, J. & de Cruz, H. (2020). *The Challenge of Evolution to Religion*. Cambridge: Cambridge University Press.

Delisle, R. G. (2017). From Charles Darwin to the evolutionary synthesis: Weak and diffused connections only. In R. G. Delisle (ed.), *The Darwinian Tradition in Context: Research Programs in Evolutionary Biology* (pp. 133–167). Cham: Springer.

Delisle, R. G. & Tierney, J. (2022). *Rereading Darwin's Origin of Species: The Hesitations of an Evolutionist*. London: Bloomsbury Academic.

Dennett, D. C. (1995). *Darwin's Dangerous Idea: Evolution and the Meanings of Life*. Harmondsworth: Penguin.

Depew, D. J. & Weber, B. H. (1995). *Darwinism Evolving: Systems Dynamics and the Genealogy of Natural Selection*. Cambridge, MA: MIT Press.

Derry, J. F. (2009). Darwin in disguise. *Trends in Ecology and Evolution* 24: 73–79.

Desmond, H., Ariew, A., Huneman, P., & Reydon, T. A. C. (2024). The varieties of Darwinism: Explanation, logic, and world-view. *Quarterly Review of Biology* 99: 77–98.

Diamond, J. (1997). *Guns, Germs, and Steel: The Fates of Human Societies*. New York: W.W. Norton & Company.

Du Crest, A., Valkovic, M., Ariew, A., Desmond, H., Huneman, P., & Reydon, T. A. C. (eds.) (2023). *Evolutionary Thinking Across Disciplines: Problems and Perspectives in Generalized Darwinism*. Cham: Springer.

Dupré, J. (2000). What the theory of evolution can't tell us. *Critical Quarterly* 42: 18–34.

Dupré, J. (2001). *Human Nature and the Limits of Science*. Oxford: Clarendon Press.

Dupré, J. (2003). *Darwin's Legacy: What Evolution Means Today*. New York: Oxford University Press.

Eiben, A. E. & Smith, J. (2015). From evolutionary computation to the evolution of things. *Nature* 521: 476–482.

Falk, R. (2009). *Genetic Analysis: A History of Genetic Thinking*. Cambridge: Cambridge University Press.

Fleck, L. (1979 [1935]). *Genesis and Development of a Scientific Fact*. Chicago: University of Chicago Press.

Fogarty, L., Kandler, A., Creanza, N., & Feldman, M. W. (2024) Half a century of quantitative cultural evolution. *Proceedings of the National Academy of Sciences of the United States of America* 121: e2418106121.

Fortuna, M. A. (2022). The phenotypic plasticity of an evolving digital organism. *Royal Society Open Science* 9: 220852.

Fracchia, J. & Lewontin, R. C. (1999). Does culture evolve? *History and Theory* 38: 52–78.

Fracchia, J. & Lewontin, R. C. (2005). The price of metaphor. *History and Theory* 44: 14–29.

French, S. (2020). *There Are No Such Things as Theories*. Oxford: Oxford University Press.

Frigg, R. (2023). *Models and Theories: A Philosophical Inquiry*. London: Routledge.

Gardner, A. (2020). Price's equation made clear. *Philosophical Transactions of the Royal Society B* 375: 20190361.

Gardner, A. & Conlon. J. P. (2013). Cosmological natural selection and the purpose of the universe. *Complexity* 18: 48–56.

Geher, G., Fritche, M., Goodwine, A., Lombard, J., Longo, K., & Montana, D. (2023). *An Introduction to Positive Evolutionary Psychology*. Cambridge: Cambridge University Press.

Gildenhuys, P. (2024). Natural selection. In E. N. Zalta & U. Nodelman (eds.), *Stanford Encyclopedia of Philosophy* (Spring 2024 Edition). https://plato.stanford.edu/archives/spr2024/entries/natural-selection/.

Gluckman, P. & Hanson, M. (2006). *Mismatch: Why Our World No Longer Fits Our Bodies*. Oxford: Oxford University Press.

Godfrey-Smith, P. (2007). Conditions for evolution by natural selection. *Journal of Philosophy* 104: 489–516.

Godfrey-Smith, P. (2009). *Darwinian Populations and Natural Selection*. Oxford: Oxford University Press.

Gontier, N. & Bradie, M. (2021). Evolutionary epistemology: Two research avenues, three schools, and a single and shared agenda. *Journal for General Philosophy of Science* 52: 197–209.

Gould, S. J. (1976). Biological determinism vs. biological potential. *Natural History* 85(5): 12–22.

Gould, S. J. (1977). *Ontogeny and Phylogeny*. Cambridge, MA: Harvard University Press.

Grüne-Yanoff, T. & Mäki, U. (2014): Introduction: Interdisciplinary model exchanges. *Studies in History and Philosophy of Science* 48: 52–59.

Hacking, I. (2002). *Historical Ontology*. Cambridge, MA: Harvard University Press.

Hamilton, W. D. (1963). The evolution of altruistic behavior. *American Naturalist* 97: 354–356.

Hannon, E. & Lewens, T. (eds.) (2018). *Why We Disagree About Human Nature*. Oxford: Oxford University Press.

Haufe, C. (2022). *How Knowledge Grows: The Evolutionary Development of Scientific Practice*. Cambridge, MA: MIT Press.

Heams, T., Huneman, P., Lecointre, G., & Silberstein, M. (eds.) (2015). *Handbook of Evolutionary Thinking in the Sciences*. Dordrecht: Springer.

Herfeld, C. (2025). Model transfer in science. In T. Knuuttila, N. Carrillo, & R. Koskinen (eds.), *The Routledge Handbook of Philosophy of Scientific Modeling* (pp. 270–283). London: Routledge.

Herfeld, C. & Lisciandra, C. (eds.) (2019). Knowledge transfer and its contexts. *Studies in History and Philosophy of Science* 77: 1–140 (special issue).

Hey, J. (2011). Regarding the confusion between the population concept and Mayr's "population thinking." *Quarterly Review of Biology* 86: 253–264.

Hodgson, G. M. (2003). The mystery of the routine: The Darwinian destiny of an evolutionary theory of economic change. *Revue Économique* 54: 355–384.

Hodgson, G. M. (2009). Introduction. In G. M. Hodgson (ed.), *Darwinism and Economics* (pp. xi–xxxvi). Cheltenham: Edward Elgar.

Hodgson, G. M. (2019). *Evolutionary Economics: Its Nature and Future*. Cambridge: Cambridge University Press.

Hodgson, G. M. & Knudsen, T. (2006). Why we need a Generalized Darwinism and why a Generalized Darwinism is not enough. *Journal of Economic Behavior and Organization* 61: 1–19.

Hodgson, G. M. & Knudsen, T. (2008). In search of general evolutionary principles: Why Darwinism is too important to be left to the biologists. *Journal of Bioeconomics* 10: 51–69.

Hodgson, G. M. & Knudsen, T. (2010). *Darwin's Conjecture: The Search for General Principles of Social and Economic Evolution*. Chicago: University of Chicago Press.

Hoquet, T. (2018). *Revisiting the Origin of Species: The Other Darwins*. London: Routledge.

Houkes, W. (2023). Embedding and customizing templates in cross-disciplinary modeling. *Synthese* 201: 79.

Houkes, W. & Zwart, S. D. (2019). Transfer and templates in scientific modelling. *Studies in History and Philosophy of Science* 77: 93–100.

Hull, D. L. (1980). Individuality and selection. *Annual Review of Ecology and Systematics* 11: 311–332.

Hull, D. L. (1981). Units of evolution: A metaphysical essay. In U. J. Jensen & R. Harré (eds.), *The Philosophy of Evolution* (pp. 23–44). Brighton: Harvester Press.

Hull, D. L. (1988). *Science as a Process: An Evolutionary Account of the Social and Conceptual Development of Science*. Chicago: University of Chicago Press.

Hull, D. L. (1998). Book review of O'Hear, Beyond Evolution. *British Journal for the Philosophy of Science* 49: 511–514.

Humphreys, P. (2019). Knowledge transfer across scientific disciplines. *Studies in History and Philosophy of Science* 77: 112–119.

Humphreys, P. & Lin, C.-H. (eds.) (2023). Transdisciplinary model and template transfer. *Synthese* (topical collection).

Huneman, P. (2010). Assessing the prospects for a return of organisms in evolutionary biology. *History and Philosophy of the Life Sciences* 32: 341–372.

Huneman, P. (2017). Why would we call for a new evolutionary synthesis? The variation issue and the explanatory alternatives. In P. Huneman & D. M. Walsh (eds.), *Challenging the Modern Synthesis: Adaptation, Development, and Inheritance* (pp. 68–110). New York: Oxford University Press.

Huneman, P. & Walsh, D. M. (eds.) (2017). *Challenging the Modern Synthesis: Adaptation, Development, and Inheritance.* New York: Oxford University Press.

Huxley, J. (1942). *Evolution: The Modern Synthesis.* London: George Allen & Unwin.

Isenberg, A. C. (2014). Introduction: A new environmental history. In A. C. Isenberg (ed.), *The Oxford Handbook of Environmental History* (pp. 1–20). Oxford: Oxford University Press.

Jablonka, E. & Lamb, M. J. (2005). *Evolution in Four Dimensions: Genetic, Epigenetic, Behavioral, and Symbolic Variation in the History of Life.* Cambridge, MA: MIT Press.

Jablonka, E. & Lamb, M. J. (2020). *Inheritance Systems and the Extended Evolutionary Synthesis.* Cambridge: Cambridge University Press.

Jacob, F. (1977). Evolution and tinkering. *Science* 196: 1161–1166.

James, W. (1890). *The Principles of Psychology, Volume I.* New York: Henry Holt and Company.

Jensen, J. D., Payseur, B. A., Stephan, W., Aquadro, C. F., Lynch, M., Charlesworth, D., & Charlesworth, B. (2019). The importance of the Neutral Theory in 1968 and 50 years on: A response to Kern and Hahn 2018. *Evolution* 73: 111–114.

Johannsen, W. (1923). Some remarks about units in heredity. *Hereditas* 4: 133–141.

Kern, A. D. & Hahn, M. W. (2018). The neutral theory in light of natural selection. *Molecular Biology and Evolution* 35: 1366–1371.

Kimura, M. (1968). Evolutionary rate at the molecular level. *Nature* 217: 624–626.

Kimura, M. (1983). *The Neutral Theory of Molecular Evolution.* Cambridge: Cambridge University Press.

King, J. L. & Jukes, T. H. (1969). Non-Darwinian evolution. *Science* 164: 788–798.

Kitcher, P. (1985). *Vaulting Ambition: Sociobiology and the Quest for Human Nature.* Cambridge, MA: MIT Press.

Knuuttila, T. & Loettgers, A. (2014). Magnets, spins, and neurons: The dissemination of model templates across disciplines. *The Monist* 97: 280–300.

Knuuttila, T. & Loettgers, A. (2016). Model templates within and between disciplines from magnets to gases – and socio-economic systems. *European Journal for the Philosophy of Science* 6: 377–400.

Knuuttila, T. & Loettgers, A. (2017). Modelling as indirect representation? The Lotka–Volterra model revisited. *British Journal for the Philosophy of Science* 68: 1007–1036.

Knuuttila, T. & Loettgers, A. (2020). Magnetized memories: Analogies and templates in model transfer. In S. Holm (ed.), *Living Machines? Philosophical Perspectives on the Engineering Approach in Biology* (pp. 123–140). London: Routledge.

Koliofotis, V. (2021). Applying evolutionary methods in economics: Progress or pitfall? *Journal of Bioeconomics* 23: 203–223.

Koonin, E. V. & Wolf, Y. I. (2009). Is evolution Darwinian or/and Lamarckian? *Biology Direct* 4: 42.

Kuhlmann, M. (2019). Crossing boundaries: Why physics can help understand economics. In B. Falkenburg & G. Schiemann (eds.), *Mechanistic Explanations in Physics and Beyond* (pp. 183–205). Cham: Springer.

Kurzban, R. & Haselton, M. G. (2006). Making hay out of straw? Real and imagined controversies in evolutionary psychology. In J. H. Barkow (ed.), *Missing the Revolution: Darwinism for Social Scientists* (pp. 149–161). New York: Oxford University Press.

Lacal, I. & Ventura, R. (2018). Epigenetic inheritance: Concepts, mechanisms and perspectives. *Frontiers in Molecular Neuroscience* 11: 292.

Lala, K. N., Uller, T., Feiner, N., Feldman, M. W., & Gilbert, S. F. (2024). *Evolution Evolving: The Developmental Origins of Adaptation and Biodiversity*. Princeton: Princeton University Press.

Laland, K. N. et al. (2014). Does evolutionary theory need a rethink? *Nature* 514: 161–164.

Laland, K. N., Uller, T., Feldman, M. W., Sterelny, K., Müller, G. B., Moczek, A., Jablonka, E., & Odling-Smee, J. (2015). The extended evolutionary synthesis: Its structure, assumptions and predictions. *Proceedings of the Royal Society B* 282: 20151019.

Larsen, M. & Witoszek, N. (2024). *Evolutionary Perspectives on Enhancing the Quality of Life*. Cambridge: Cambridge University Press.

LeGrand, E. K. & Brown, C. C. (2002). Darwinian medicine: Applications of evolutionary biology for veterinarians. *The Canadian Veterinary Journal* 43: 556–559.

Lemmon, R. M. (1970). Chemical evolution. *Chemical Reviews* 70: 95–109.

Lenhard, J. & Hasse, H. (2023). Traveling with TARDIS. Parameterization and transferability in molecular modeling and simulation. *Synthese* 201: 129.

Lenski, R. E., Ofria, C., Pennock, R. T., & Adami, C. (2003). The evolutionary origins of complex features. *Nature* 423: 139–144.

Leopold, A. (1949). *A Sand County Almanac and Sketches Here and There*. New York: Oxford University Press.

Levit, G. S. & Olsson, L. (2006). "Evolution on rails": Mechanisms and levels of orthogenesis. *Annals for the History and Philosophy of Biology* 11: 97–136.

Levit, G. S., Meister, K., & Hoßfeld, U. (2008). Alternative evolutionary theories: A historical survey. *Journal of Bioeconomics* 10: 71–96.

Lewens, T. (2007). *Darwin*. London: Routledge.

Lewens, T. (2010). Natural selection then and now. *Biological Reviews* 85: 829–835.

Lewens, T. (2015). *Cultural Evolution: Conceptual Challenges*. Oxford: Oxford University Press.

Lewens, T. (2019). The Extended Evolutionary Synthesis: What is the debate about, and what might success for the extenders look like? *Biological Journal of the Linnean Society* 127: 707–721.

Lewens, T. (2024). *Cultural Selection*. Cambridge: Cambridge University Press.

Lewontin, R. C. (1970). The units of selection. *Annual Review of Ecology and Systematics* 1: 1–18.

Lewontin, R. C. (1980). Sociobiology: Another biological determinism. *International Journal of Health Services* 10: 347–363.

Lewontin, R. C. (1991). The structure and confirmation of evolutionary theory. *Biology & Philosophy* 6: 461–466.

Lewontin, R. C. (2010). Not so natural selection. *The New York Review of Books* LVII, Nr. 9 (May 27, 2010). www.nybooks.com/articles/archives/2010/may/27/not-so-natural-selection/.

Li, N. P., Van Vught, M., & Colarelli, S. M. (2018). The evolutionary mismatch hypothesis: Implications for psychological science. *Current Directions in Psychological Science* 27: 38–44.

Liepman, H. P. (1981). The six editions of the 'Origin of Species'. *Acta Biotheoretica* 30: 199–214.

Love, A. C. (2019). Evolution evolving? Reflections on big questions. *Journal of Experimental Zoology B: Molecular and Developmental Evolution* 332: 315–320.

Love, A. C. (2024). *Evolution and Development*. Cambridge: Cambridge University Press.

Luque, V. J. (2016). Drift and evolutionary forces: Scrutinizing the Newtonian analogy. *Theoria* 31: 397–410.

Maasen, S., Mendelsohn, E., & Weingart, P. (eds.) (1995). *Biology as Society, Society as Biology: Metaphors*. Dordrecht: Kluwer Academic Publishers.

Mameli, M. & Bateson, P. (2006). Innateness and the sciences. *Biology & Philosophy* 21: 155–188.

Maschner, H. D. G. & Mithen, S. (1996). Darwinian archaeologies: An introductory essay. In H. D. G. Maschner (ed.), *Darwinian Archaeologies* (pp. 3–14). New York: Plenum Press.

Maynard Smith, J., Burian, R., Kauffman, S., Alberch, P., Campbell, J., Goodwin, B., Lande, R., Raup, D., & Wolpert, L. (1985). Developmental constraints and evolution: A perspective from the Mountain Lake Conference on Development and Evolution. *Quarterly Review of Biology* 60: 265–287.

Mayntz, R. (1992). The influence of natural science theories on contemporary social science. In M. Dierkes & B. Biervert (eds.), *European Social Science in Transition: Assessment and Outlook* (pp. 27–79). Boulder, CO: Westview Press.

Mayntz, R. (1997a). *Soziale Dynamik und politische Steuerung: Theoretische und methodologische Überlegungen*. Frankfurt am Main: Campus.

Mayntz, R. (1997b). Chaos in society: Reflections on the impact of chaos theory on sociology. In C. Grebogi & J. A. Yorke (eds.), *The Impact of Chaos on Science and Society* (pp. 298–323). Tokyo: United Nations University Press.

Mayr, E. (1980). Prologue: Some thoughts on the history of the evolutionary synthesis. In E. Mayr & W. B. Provine (eds.), *The Evolutionary Synthesis: Perspectives on the Unification of Biology* (pp. 1–48). Cambridge, MA: Harvard University Press.

Mayr, E. (1985). Darwin's five theories of evolution. In D. Kohn (ed.), *The Darwinian Heritage* (pp. 755–772). Princeton: Princeton University Press.

Mazur, A. (1978). Biological explanation in sociology. *Sociological Quarterly* 19: 604–613.

McGuire, M. & Troisi, A. (1998). *Darwinian Psychiatry*. New York: Oxford University Press.

McLoone, B. (2022). Natural selection's explanatory scope. *Philosophy Compass* 17: e12881.

Mesoudi, A. (2011). *Cultural Evolution: How Darwinian Theory Can Explain Human Culture and Synthesize the Social Sciences*. Chicago: University of Chicago Press.

Midgley, M. (2002). *Evolution as a Religion: Strange Hopes and Stranger Fears (Revised Edition)*. London: Routledge.

Miikulainen, R. & Forrest, S. (2021). A biological perspective on evolutionary computation. *Nature Machine Intelligence* 3: 9–15.

Millstein, R. L. (2009). Populations as individuals. *Biological Theory* 4: 267–273.

Millstein, R. L. (2010). The concepts of population and metapopulation in evolutionary biology and ecology. In M. A. Bell, D. J. Futuyma, W. F. Eanes, & J. S. Levinton (eds.), *Evolution Since Darwin: The First 150 Years* (pp. 61–86). Sunderland, MA: Sinauer.

Millstein, R. L. (2024). *The Land Is Our Community: Aldo Leopold's Environmental Ethic for the New Millennium*. Chicago: University of Chicago Press.

Mitchell, M. & Taylor, C. E. (1999). Evolutionary computation: An overview. *Annual Review of Ecology and Systematics* 30: 593–616.

Müller, G. B. & Newman, S. A. (2003). Origination of organismal form: The forgotten cause in evolutionary theory. In G. B. Müller & S. A. Newman (eds.), *Origination of Organismal Form: Beyond the Gene in Developmental and Evolutionary Biology* (pp. 3–10). Cambridge, MA: MIT Press.

Nelson, R. R. (2007). Universal Darwinism and evolutionary social science. *Biology & Philosophy* 22: 73–94.

Nelson, R. R. (2018). Economics from an evolutionary perspective. In R. R. Nelson, G. Dosi, C. E. Helfat, A. Pyka, S. G. Winter, P. P. Saviotti, K. Lee, F. Malerba, & K. Dopfer, *Modern Evolutionary Economics: An Overview* (pp. 1–34). Cambridge: Cambridge University Press.

Nelson, R. R. & Winter, S. G. (1982). *An Evolutionary Theory of Economic Change*. Cambridge, MA: Harvard University Press.

Nesse, R. N. & Williams, G. C. (1994). *Why We Get Sick: The New Science of Darwinian Medicine*. New York: Random House.

Nichols, R., Charbonneau, M., Chellappoo, A., Davis, T., Haidle, M., Kimbrough, E. O., Moll, H., Moore, R., Scott-Phillips, T., Purzycki, B. G., & Segovia-Martin, J. (2024). Cultural evolution: A review of theoretical challenges. *Evolutionary Human Sciences* 6: e12.

Nicholson, D. J. (2014). The return of the organism as a fundamental explanatory concept in biology. *Philosophy Compass* 9: 347–359.

Nicoglou, A. (2024). *Plasticity in the Life Sciences*. Chicago: University of Chicago Press.

Nowak, M. A. (2006a). *Evolutionary Dynamics: Exploring the Equations of Life*. Cambridge, MA: Harvard University Press.

Nowak, M. A. (2006b). Five rules for the evolution of cooperation. *Science* 314: 1560–1563.

O'Connell, J. & Ruse, M. (2021). *Social Darwinism*. Cambridge: Cambridge University Press.

Odling-Smee, F. J., Laland, K. N., & Feldman, M. W. (2003). *Niche Construction: The Neglected Process in Evolution*. Princeton: Princeton University Press.

Okasha, S. (2001). Why won't the group selection controversy go away? *British Journal for the Philosophy of Science* 52: 25–50.

Okasha, S. (2006). The levels of selection debate: Philosophical issues. *Philosophy Compass* 1: 74–85.

Papale, F. (2021). Evolution by means of natural selection without reproduction: Revamping Lewontin's account. *Synthese* 198: 10429–10455.

Partridge, D. (2018). Darwin's two theories, 1844 and 1859. *Journal of the History of Biology* 51: 563–592.

Pence, C. H. (2021). *The Causal Structure of Natural Selection*. Cambridge: Cambridge University Press.

Pennock, R. T. (2016). Evolution and computing. In J. B. Losos & R. E. Lenski (eds.), *How Evolution Shapes Our Lives: Essays on Biology and Society* (pp. 206–219). Princeton: Princeton University Press.

Pigliucci, M. & Müller, G. B. (2010). Elements of an extended evolutionary synthesis. In M. Pigliucci & G. B. Müller (eds.), *Evolution: The Extended Synthesis* (pp. 3–17). Cambridge, MA: MIT Press.

Prentiss, A. M. (2021). Theoretical plurality, the extended evolutionary synthesis, and archaeology. *Proceedings of the National Academy of Sciences of the United States of America* 118: e2006564118.

Ramsey, G. (2023). *Human Nature*. Cambridge: Cambridge University Press.

Reydon, T. A. C. (2011). The arrival of the fittest *what*? In D. Dieks, W. J. Gonzalez, S. Hartmann, T. Uebel, & M. Weber (eds.), *Explanation, Prediction, and Confirmation* (pp. 223–237). Dordrecht: Springer.

Reydon, T. A. C. (2015). The evolution of human nature and its implications for politics: A critique. *Journal of Bioeconomics* 17: 17–36.

Reydon, T. A. C. (2021). Generalized Darwinism as modest unification. *American Philosophical Quarterly* 58: 79–93.

Reydon, T. A. C. (2023). The proper role of history in evolutionary explanations. *Noûs* 57: 162–187.

Reydon, T. A. C. & Scholz, M. (2009). Why organizational ecology is not a Darwinian research program. *Philosophy of the Social Sciences* 39: 408–439.

Reydon, T. A. C. & Scholz, M. (2014). Darwinism and Organizational Ecology: A case of in-completeness or incompatibility? *Philosophy of the Social Sciences* 44: 364–373.

Reydon, T. A. C. & Scholz, M. (2015). Searching for Darwinism in Generalized Darwinism. *British Journal for the Philosophy of Science* 66: 561–589.

Rickles, D. (2007). Econophysics for philosophers. *Studies in History and Philosophy of Modern Physics* 38: 948–978.

Romanes, G. J. (1892). *Darwin, and after Darwin: An Exposition of the Darwinian Theory and a Discussion of Post-Darwinian Questions I: The Darwinian Theory.* Chicago: The Open Court Publishing Company.

Romanes, G. J. (1895). *Darwin, and after Darwin: An Exposition of the Darwinian Theory and a Discussion of Post-Darwinian Questions II: Post-Darwinian Questions, Heredity and Utility.* Chicago: The Open Court Publishing Company.

Rubin, H. (2024). *Inclusive Fitness and Kin Selection.* Cambridge: Cambridge University Press.

Ruse, M. (2005). *The Evolution-Creation Struggle.* Cambridge, MA: Harvard University Press.

Ruse, M. (2017). *Darwinism as Religion: What Literature Tells Us About Evolution.* New York: Oxford University Press.

Ruse, M. (2023). *Understanding Natural Selection.* Cambridge: Cambridge University Press.

Ruse, M. & Richards, R. J. (eds.) (2017). *The Cambridge Handbook of Evolutionary Ethics.* Cambridge: Cambridge University Press.

Ruse, M. & Wilson, E. O. (1986). Moral philosophy as applied science. *Philosophy* 61: 173–192.

Russell, E. (2003). Evolutionary history: Prospectus for a new field. *Environmental History* 8: 204–228.

Russell, E. (2011). *Evolutionary History: Uniting History and Biology to Understand Life on Earth.* Cambridge: Cambridge University Press.

Schoenauer, M. (2015). Evolutionary algorithms. In T. Heams, P. Huneman, G. Lecointre, & M. Silberstein (eds.), *Handbook of Evolutionary Thinking in the Sciences* (pp. 621–635). Dordrecht: Springer.

Schoenmakers, L., Reydon, T. A. C., & Kirschning, A. (2024). Evolution at the origins of life? *Life* 14: 175.

Scholz, M. & Reydon, T. A. C. (2013). On the explanatory power of Generalized Darwinism: Missing items on the research agenda. *Organization Studies* 34: 993–999.

Schulz, A. (2020). *Structure, Evidence, and Heuristic: Evolutionary Biology, Economics, and the Philosophy of Their Relationship.* New York: Routledge.

Schurz, G. (2011). *Evolution in Natur und Kultur: Eine Einführung in die verallgemeinerte Evolutionstheorie.* Heidelberg: Spektrum Akademischer Verlag.

Schwab, I. (2018). The evolution of eyes: Major steps. *Eye* 32: 302–313.

Sciortino, L. (2017). On Ian Hacking's notion of style of reasoning. *Erkenntnis* 82: 243–264.

Segerstråle, U. (2000) *Defenders of the Truth: The Sociobiology Debate*. Oxford: Oxford University Press.

Sella, G. & Hirsh, A. E. (2005). The application of statistical physics to evolutionary biology. *Proceedings of the National Academy of Sciences of the United States of America* 102: 9541–9546.

Skipper, R. A. & Millstein, R. L. (2005). Thinking about evolutionary mechanisms: Natural selection. *Studies in History and Philosophy of Biological and Biomedical Sciences* 36: 327–347.

Smaldino, P. E. (2022). Five models of science, illustrating how selection shapes methods. In G. Ramsey & A. De Block (eds.), *The Dynamics of Science: Computational Frontiers in History and Philosophy of Science* (pp. 19–39). Pittsburgh: University of Pittsburgh Press.

Smaldino, P. E. & McElreath, R. (2016). The natural selection of bad science. *Royal Society Open Science* 3: 160384.

Smith, S. E. (2020). Is evolutionary psychology possible? *Biological Theory* 15: 39–49.

Smocovitis, V. B. (1992). Unifying biology: The evolutionary synthesis and evolutionary biology. *Journal of the History of Biology* 25: 1–65.

Smocovitis, V. B. (1996). *Unifying Biology: The Evolutionary Synthesis and Evolutionary Biology*. Princeton: Princeton University Press.

Smolin, L. (1992). Did the universe evolve? *Classical and Quantum Gravity* 9: 173–191.

Sober, E. (1984). *The Nature of Selection: Evolutionary Theory in Philosophical Focus*. Chicago: University of Chicago Press.

Sober, E. (2009). Did Darwin write the *Origin* backwards? *Proceedings of the National Academy of Sciences of the United States of America* 106: 10048–10055.

Sober, E. & Wilson, D. S. (1998). *Unto Others: The Evolution and Psychology of Unselfish Behaviors*. Cambridge, MA: Harvard University Press.

Spencer, H. (1890). *First Principles (A System of Synthetic Philosophy, Vol. I)*. New York: D. Appleton and Company.

Spencer, H. (1891). *Essays: Scientific, Political, & Speculative, Vol. I*. London: Williams and Norgate.

Stauffer, R. C. (ed.) (1975). *Charles Darwin's Natural Selection, Being the Second Part of His Big Species Book Written From 1856 to 1858*. Cambridge: Cambridge University Press.

Stegmann, U. (2010). What can natural selection explain? *Studies in History and Philosophy of Biological and Biomedical Sciences* 41: 61–66.

Stoelhorst, J. W. (2008a). The explanatory logic and ontological commitments of generalized Darwinism. *Journal of Economic Methodology* 15: 343–363.

Stoelhorst, J. W. (2008b). Darwinian foundations for evolutionary economics. *Journal of Economic Issues* 42: 415–423.

Tieleman, S. (2022). Model transfer and universal patterns: Lessons from the Yule process. *Synthese* 200: 267.

Tooby, L. & Cosmides, L. (1990). The past explains the present: Emotional adaptations and the structure of ancestral environments. *Ethology and Sociobiology* 11: 375–424.

Trivers, R. (1971). The evolution of reciprocal altruism. *Quarterly Review of Biology* 46: 35–57.

Vavova, K. (2015) Evolutionary debunking of moral realism. *Philosophy Compass* 10: 104–116.

Veblen, T. B. (1898). Why is economics not an evolutionary science? *Quarterly Journal of Economics* 12: 373–397.

Veit, W. & Browning, H. (2023). Developmental programming, evolution, and animal welfare: A case for evolutionary veterinary science. *Journal of Applied Animal Welfare Science* 26: 552–564.

Wallace, A. R. (1889). *Darwinism: An Exposition of the Theory of Natural Selection with Some of Its Applications*. London: Macmillan and Co.

Walsh, D. M. (2010). Two neo-Darwinisms. *History and Philosophy of the Life Sciences* 32: 317–340.

Walsh, D. M. (2012). The struggle for life and the conditions of existence: Two interpretation of Darwinian evolution. In M. Brinkworth & F. Weinert (eds), *Evolution 2.0: Implications of Darwinism in Philosophy and the Social and Natural Sciences* (pp. 191–209). Berlin & Heidelberg: Springer.

Walsh, D. M., Lewens, T., & Ariew, A. (2002). The trials of life: Natural selection and random drift. *Philosophy of Science* 69: 452–473.

Walsh, D. M., Ariew, A., & Matthen, M. (2017). Four pillars of statisticalism. *Philosophy, Theory, and Practice in Biology* 9: 1.

Weismann, A. (1893). The all-sufficiency of natural selection. *Contemporary Review* 64: 309–338.

West-Eberhard, M. J. (2003). *Developmental Plasticity and Evolution*. New York: Oxford University Press.

White, R. M., Hodge, M. J. S., & Radick, G. (2021). *Darwin's Argument by Analogy: From Artificial to Natural Selection*. Cambridge: Cambridge University Press.

Wilke, C. O. & Adami, C. (2002). The biology of digital organisms. *Trends in Ecology & Evolution* 17: 528–532.

Wilkins, J. S. & Bourrat, P. (2022). Replication and reproduction, In E. N. Zalta & U. Nodelman (eds.), *Stanford Encyclopedia of Philosophy*

(Winter 2022 Edition). https://plato.stanford.edu/archives/win2022/entries/replication/.
Williams, G. C. & Nesse, R. N. (1991). The dawn of Darwinian medicine. *Quarterly Review of Biology* 66: 1–22.
Wilson, D. S. (2002). *Darwin's Cathedral: Evolution, Religion, and the Nature of Society*. Chicago: University of Chicago Press.
Wilson, D. S. (2007). *Evolution for Everyone*. New York: Delacorte Press.
Wilson, D. S. (2011). *The Neighborhood Project: Using Evolution to Improve My City, One Block at a Time*. New York: Little, Brown and Company.
Wilson, D. S. (2019). *This View of Life: Completing the Darwinian Revolution*. New York: Pantheon Books.
Wilson. E. O. (1975). *Sociobiology: The New Synthesis*. Cambridge, MA: Harvard University Press.
Wilson, E. O. (2016). The meaning of human existence. In J. Carroll, D. P. McAdams, & E. O. Wilson (eds.), *Darwin's Bridge: Uniting the Humanities & Sciences* (pp. 3–7). New York: Oxford University Press.
Winfield, A. F. T. (2024). Evolutionary robotics as a modelling tool in evolutionary biology. *Frontiers in Robotics and AI* 11: 1278983.
Winther, R. G. (2021). The structure of scientific theories. In E. N. Zalta (ed.), *Stanford Encyclopedia of Philosophy* (Spring 2021 Edition). https://plato.stanford.edu/archives/spr2021/entries/structure-scientific-theories/.
Woodward, J. & Ross, L. (2021). Scientific explanation. In E. N. Zalta (ed.), *Stanford Encyclopedia of Philosophy* (Summer 2021 Edition). https://plato.stanford.edu/archives/sum2021/entries/scientific-explanation/.
Yee, A. K. (2021). Econophysics: Making sense of a chimera. *European Journal for Philosophy of Science* 11: 100.
Ziemke, T., Bergfeldt, N., Buason, G., Susi, T., & Svensson, H. (2004). Evolving cognitive scaffolding and environment adaptation: A new research direction for evolutionary robotics. *Connection Science* 16: 339–350.
Ziman, J. (ed.) (2000). *Technological Innovation as an Evolutionary Process*. Cambridge: Cambridge University Press.
Zurek, W. H. (2009). Quantum Darwinism. *Nature Physics* 5: 181–188.

Acknowledgments

For their many helpful comments on the manuscript, I am indebted to Karim Baraghith, Hugh Desmond, Philippe Huneman, Simon Lohse, Ludo Schoenmakers, Jan-Willem Stoelhorst, and two anonymous reviewers for the press. Research for this Element was supported by a joint grant from the *Deutsche Forschungsgemeinschaft* (DFG) and the *Agence Nationale de la Recherche* (ANR) that funded a project I led jointly with Philippe Huneman (*The Explanatory Scope of Generalized Darwinism: Towards Criteria for Evolutionary Explanations Outside Biology*; DFG project nr. 430626147). This publication received financial support from the Open Access Fund of *Leibniz Universität Hannover*.

Cambridge Elements ≡

Philosophy of Biology

Grant Ramsey
KU Leuven

Grant Ramsey is a BOFZAP research professor at the Institute of Philosophy, KU Leuven, Belgium. His work centers on philosophical problems at the foundation of evolutionary biology. He has been awarded the Popper Prize twice for his work in this area. He also publishes in the philosophy of animal behavior, human nature, and the moral emotions. He runs the Ramsey Lab (theramseylab.org), a highly collaborative research group focused on issues in the philosophy of the life sciences.

About the Series

This Cambridge Elements series provides concise and structured introductions to all of the central topics in the philosophy of biology. Contributors to the series are cutting-edge researchers who offer balanced, comprehensive coverage of multiple perspectives, while also developing new ideas and arguments from a unique viewpoint.

Cambridge Elements

Philosophy of Biology

Elements in the Series

Evolution and Development: Conceptual Issues
Alan C. Love

Inclusive Fitness and Kin Selection
Hannah Rubin

Animal Models of Human Disease
Sara Green

Cultural Selection
Tim Lewens

Biological Organization
Leonardo Bich

Controlled Experiments
Jutta Schickore

Slime Mould and Philosophy
Matthew Sims

Explanation in Biology
Lauren N. Ross

Philosophy of Physiology
Maël Lemoine

The Organism
Jan Baedke

Human Cognitive Diversity
Ingo Brigandt

The Scope of Evolutionary Thinking
Thomas A. C. Reydon

A full series listing is available at: www.cambridge.org/EPBY

Made in the USA
Monee, IL
03 May 2026

49437835R00056